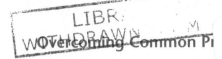

Overcoming Common Problems

Overcoming Common Problems Series

Dealing with dysfunctional relationships

TOXIC PEOPLE

sheldon^{PRESS}

Dr TIM CANTOPHER

First published in Great Britain in 2017

Sheldon Press
36 Causton Street
London SW1P 4ST
www.sheldonpress.co.uk

British Library Cataloguing-in-Publication Data
A catalogue record for this book is available from the British Library

ISBN 978-1-84709-435-3
eBook ISBN 978-1-84709-436-0

1 3 5 7 9 10 8 6 4 2

Typeset by Fakenham Prepress Solutions, Fakenham, Norfolk NR21 8NN
Printed in Great Britain by Ashford Colour Press

eBook by Fakenham Prepress Solutions, Fakenham, Norfolk NR21 8NN

Produced on paper from sustainable forests

To Laura, the most healing person I know

Contents

Acknowledgements

I am indebted to Dr Loretta Rittenhouse for her helpful feedback and suggestions, to my wife Laura for proof-reading and suggesting appropriate names for the characters in the book, to the team at Sheldon for their enthusiastic and patient support, to the Royal Society of Medicine for use of their excellent library facilities and to Mr Donald Trump for being such a good model for almost all of the personalities described in Chapter 4.

A note to the reader

This is not a medical book and is not intended to replace advice from your doctor. Consult your pharmacist or doctor if you believe you have any of the symptoms described, and if you think you might need medical help.

Introduction

'No I can't. I just haven't got time, honestly. I have to take my mother to the hospital, then run errands for my husband and then make the dinner.'

Helen doesn't know whether she's coming or going, and her friend Anita is giving her a hard time because she was hoping Helen would look after her five-year-old son, allowing Anita a night out with her husband.

'Oh well, if keeping your mum and your husband happy are more important than me, that's how it is I suppose. I'm surprised though; I would have thought you'd try to make it work for your best friend, after all I've done for you. You should stand up to your mum and stop being such a doormat for that husband of yours.'

Helen has already tried to put her mother off by offering to book a taxi for her to and from the hospital, but she was having none of it. 'If a mother can't even turn to her daughter at a time like this, when she's ill, things have come to a pretty pass. I'll be dead soon, so you won't have to worry about me. Until then I've a right to expect you to do your duty. Mark my words, you'll be sorry when I'm gone and you'll wish you'd done more.'

End of discussion.

Helen isn't even going to approach her husband Edward to give her a break. He's not the understanding sort. Being the main bread-winner, he expects everything to be done for him at home. Anyway, he loathes his mother-in-law and likes Anita rather less.

It's ironic really. Helen's mother never did care for her much as a child. She was too busy being important, being seen to do good works and being the centre of attention in the local village. The duty she expects of Helen is one she herself never felt constrained by as a mother. The same is true about Anita. The fact is Anita doesn't do anything for Helen, expecting her to be grateful to be allowed into her social circle, to be indebted and to pay her debts regularly by being at Anita's beck and call. If Helen is a doormat, Anita is the one who wipes her feet on her more than anyone. Now Helen comes to think about it, Edward is the same. When at home he largely drinks, sleeps and watches sport on TV. He is satisfied that, as a middle-ranking manager, he provides a comfortable life for Helen, and he expects her to fulfil her side of the bargain by doing as she's told and keeping things running smoothly at home. This doesn't include being unavailable because she's running errands for others.

So as always, Helen makes it work. She gets all the shopping, the errands and chores done early, she skips lunch, gets her mother to the hospital on time, sorts out the household paperwork while in the waiting room, takes her mother home, makes her a cup of tea and prepares her dinner while offering her as much reassurance as she can, given her limited medical knowledge. Just enough time to pick up her daughter Ethel from school, get to Anita's, bring her friend's son round to her house, feed him and then her own daughter (they don't like the same food, and Helen's ten-year-old is certainly not going to eat supper at the same time as someone half her age). She sets the little boy up in the spare bedroom, but since this is an unfamiliar environment it takes a while to get him off to sleep. Next it's preparing dinner for Edward. Helen doesn't eat much; she doesn't have time.

Then Edward phones to say he's going to be late home. This means Helen has to keep Ethel up late, so that when it's time to drive Anita's sleeping son back home, her daughter can go with her. Anita is cross with Helen for turning up without the boy's favourite toy. Edward arrives home and her mother calls when she's out. Both are angry that she's kept her daughter up past 10 p.m. on a weekday.

When Helen becomes exhausted and ill, she gets no sympathy, just huffing and resentful puffing from those whom she can no longer serve in the way to which they have become accustomed.

Helen is a prisoner. Some of the people around her are toxic. This book is aimed at Helen and many like her. Helen's prison is of her own making. The bars on her cell aren't made by Anita or her mother or her husband, but by Helen herself. The door to her cell is unlocked. She just needs to learn how to walk through it.

That's what this book is for. If Helen can spot toxic people, can avoid them when possible and when not, learn to cope healthily with them, she will be free. There are lots of Helens and the characters around them come in many different shapes and sizes, some operating more subtly than those in this introduction, but the result is the same. For the majority of the thousands of people who have entered my consulting room suffering from stress-related illness, the largest contributing factor was other people. There are better and healthier ways of coping with these folks. This doesn't necessarily mean leaving your husband, being un-Christian (if that is your religion) or ceasing to care about others.

I have written this book because there doesn't seem to be anything in the existing self-help literature designed to help with such issues. There is plenty on sociopaths (psychopaths) and those with other severe personality disorders, but not on people who display just a bit of these traits and are simply difficult to deal with. There is a lot on the effects of abuse and neglect, but little on the everyday unkindness, game playing and insensitivity which, if you let it, can make you ill.

That's what the pages which follow are for. I hope that they can help you to reconstruct your life in a better, happier and healthier form. You will need to take what you read with a pinch of salt though. No book can deal with every situation or nuance you face, but I hope you will find some useful pointers here. If in doubt, seek professional advice rather than following mine, or anyone else's, to the letter.

While my description of some of the types of people who inhabit these pages may sound critical, I don't mean it to be that way. People are the way they are for very good reasons, mostly to do with their own upbringings, so there's no point in blaming them for being who they are. It's up to you to find ways of staying happy and healthy, rather than relying on others to protect you. But trust me on this; life is better outside your prison.

Note: details of specific incidents described in the book, and the names of those involved, have been changed to preserve anonymity.

Part 1
HOW PEOPLE TICK

1

People

Wake up!

OK, that sounded a bit rude – sorry. Please wake up! That's better.

Most of us tend to sleepwalk through our lives, rarely making conscious decisions about what we want or how we choose our lives to be. We react to circumstances and to other people's expectations of us. That's all well and good if those people are kind and thoughtful and if life cooperates, but it isn't so good if life turns hostile or those around us aren't the generous sort. The trouble is that people who put others first tend to get surrounded by the takers of the world. The truth is that most people are quite kind most of the time, though we all have our moments. But a few people really aren't very kind at all, and they develop over the years sharp antennae enabling them to pick up those who they can use and abuse. So those who wander through life trying to please others tend to be surrounded by such individuals. You tend either to come to believe that most people are nasty or that it is your own fault. You feel that people are nasty to you because you aren't good enough. You just need to try harder to please everyone.

Wrong. What you need is to see beyond the takers who encircle you. To achieve that, you need to work out what you really want from life; and you need to understand why people behave the way they do, so that you can develop a strategy for life. So let's look at those questions.

The next three chapters contain a lot of information. It may all seem confusing and rather obscure unless you are interested in personal and social psychology, but please bear with me. An understanding of how people tick is crucial if you are going to learn how to cope with them better. The facts and theory which make up these chapters are a necessary basis from which the rest of the book follows. I think that if I can give you some of the theoretical knowledge which sociologists, therapists, psychologists and psychiatrists possess about human behaviour, you'll learn how to cope with people and situations much better. If I'm right, by the end of these chapters I shall have rendered the rest of the book fairly redundant. Once you know why people do what they do, you don't really need someone to tell you how to deal with them; it's obvious. We shall see.

This is only a smattering of what I think is most relevant in the context of what the book is trying to achieve, lifted from a vast literature on these subjects, so please forgive me if I have left out something you feel is important.

What is personality and how is it formed?

Understanding people's personalities is the key to coping with them. Personality is defined by actions. For example, if we say that someone has an extrovert personality, we mean (put simply) that that person goes out a lot. Traits of personality are dimensional. Conscience, kindness and generosity, for example, are traits held to a degree by the vast majority of people, but nobody is perfectly kind and generous to everyone all the time. Our personality traits predict quite well how we will react to a situation or person, but not with complete accuracy. Our degree of freedom to make conscious decisions in response to a person or event depends on what is going on, our mental state and the resonances (see page 7) we experience. We are more than our impulses, but only if we make an active choice to be so. Unless you actively choose to change, you will always react in the same predictable way to the people who have harmed you or to those you identified with in the past. Being a victim of toxic people is habit-forming. Helen, whom we met in the Introduction, will have to make some difficult changes to the way she lives if her life is going to get better.

Personality is formed through experiences, especially those we go through in childhood. The way a person thinks, feels and acts is determined to an extent by genetics, but is more the product of her experiences. This continuous moulding of a person's nature by the world she experiences is referred to as her psychodynamics. Freud and countless psychoanalysts since have focused on the psychodynamic factors explaining human behaviour, especially those that occur early in life though children's interactions with their parents.

In contrast, behavioural scientists have taken the approach that what primarily underpins human behaviour is conditioning. This comes in two types, *classical* and *operant* conditioning. In the classical form a stimulus is paired with a response long enough to cause the one to trigger the other. So, for Pavlov's dogs, a bell was rung every time that meat was brought for them. At first it was the sight and smell of the meat which caused the dogs to salivate, but eventually they would drool even when the bell alone was rung, whether or not meat was present. They had been conditioned to salivate to the sound of a bell. A person who has witnessed a shooting and subsequently startles every time he hears a loud noise is exhibiting the same response.

In operant conditioning the pairing of reward, or lack of it, with an action increases the frequency with which that action is performed. So a child is awarded a star every time she behaves well, but the star is withheld if her behaviour has been poor, causing her over time to behave better. In both forms of conditioning, the phenomenon of extinction occurs, meaning that if the originally paired stimuli are no longer paired, or if the reward is no longer paired with the desired behaviour, the response will eventually fade. So if you stop producing meat when the bell is rung, the dog will eventually stop salivating, the traumatized person will eventually become less jumpy and the child who is not consistently rewarded for good behaviour, or who is sometimes rewarded for bad behaviour, will eventually stop behaving well. If, however, you continue or resume the pairing or reward, the response increases (it is reinforced).

More recently psychologists have recognized the importance of thought as well as behaviours in determining how a person feels and operates. A person can be rewarded and her behaviours therefore changed just by changing the way she thinks. If, every time you speak to someone, you criticize yourself for not being clever enough, you are unlikely ever to become good in social situations. Alternatively, if you refuse to judge yourself, if you focus on the nice things the person says and enjoy the interesting parts of the conversation, the psychological reward you gain from the experience will make it more likely that you engage successfully in social situations in the future. How you think is very important and is the basis of cognitive behavioural therapy (CBT), which has been found to be a highly effective treatment for a wide range of conditions.

Personality is not set in stone. It can change depending on the different demands you face in different environments, the experiences you have during your life, and simply with the passage of time. I was a very different person at work from who I was at home. Some people who suffer brain injury undergo a drastic change of personality as a result.

In any case, personality is in the eye of the beholder, requiring a value judgement to determine it. Is the person you're dealing with assertive or a bully? Honest or tactless? Frank or cruel? The trouble is that those who have no need to make these judgements tend to do so, whereas the vulnerable people who really need to make critical evaluations of people in order to improve their situation do so only rarely. They feel that they are somehow unworthy of having this privilege.

It's usually a good idea anyway to spend more time on understanding yourself than on making judgements about others. People tend to thrive when they know what they feel, want and need, and achieve a congruence between those things and their lives. I love space, water and good weather and I'm able to take pleasure in my own company. My life (I'm retired and live just outside Charleston, in the United States of America, overlooking a river and marshland) is congruent with these traits and needs, so I'm thriving. But balance is necessary too, so although it would be easy for me to live the life of a hermit, I make myself engage in some social contact. When dealing with toxicity, it will be important to know what you need in order to thrive, and to decide on how to balance your needs with the demands you face.

In deciding how to run our lives we need to check our goals by reference to reasonable others. At the same time we need to avoid being slaves to those with the strongest opinions. I've come to realize through life that the strength of people's opinions tends to be inversely proportional to their wisdom. Late in life, Descartes wrote: 'I am here quite alone and at last will devote myself sincerely and without reservation to the general demolition of my opinions.' Now there's wisdom for you.

Identification

The actions of people which cause suffering in others make us resentful or angry, while those which do good make us grateful and admiring, even when we aren't directly affected. This is because we identify with the object of those actions. People shouldn't do harmful things, they shouldn't be like that. Why? Why should they be like you and hold your values? The answer is that we identify with others, particularly those like us, and so the things and people that affect them also affect us.

In fact, most of us tend to act first and think later. We do things, then make up justifiable reasons for our actions after the event, believing our own false reasoning. In an experiment subjects were asked to wag a finger at random intervals. Brain wave measurements showed that the motor pathways for finger-wagging were activated well before the subjects were aware that they had decided to do so. Your intentions may not be as 'good' as you make them out to be, since many of your actions have been decided before you were aware of what you had chosen to do.

If all of this seems rather confusing, it is, at least to me. The main point I want to make is that judging the rectitude or culpability of others isn't usually useful. But we do need to understand people, their motivations and their likely actions, particularly people who don't have our welfare at the top of their list of priorities. Then we can decide on strategies for avoiding coming to harm from them. If you swim in a toxic pool, wear a good dry suit and don't swallow the water.

Resonance, intention, power and punishment

Most 'bad' acts (though not those perpetrated by a psychopath or a sadist) come from a feeling of weakness. Mostly, people do things that cause others to suffer because they feel powerless in the face of a more powerful oppressor. The underdog feels she is striking a blow for freedom, whereas her victim is perplexed. 'I didn't oppress you, why are you doing this to me?' he laments. But he is missing the fact that we all symbolize others, through the phenomenon of *resonance*. This is the way in which we experience everything and everyone in the present with reference to experiences we had earlier in our lives. It isn't really you who is being attacked by the woman who is so angry with you, but her long-dead father, or the nation which she has been taught is the architect of her people's misfortune. Little comfort, I know, when you are under verbal or physical assault, but understanding that everyone's motivations and experiences are different may help you to realize that much of what happens to you really isn't about you at all. Understanding where others are coming from can help you to deal with them a lot more successfully.

I think that what is 'good' and 'bad' is actually quite difficult to sort out. The older I get, the more I realize that there are two sides to most things and the less certain I am of anything. I believe that certainty is often born of ignorance at best, and of malice at worst. There is a difference between intent and outcome, and if we make judgements based on what a person does, we may be missing the point. Is a psychopath who kills a hundred terrorists a better person than one who kills a nursing mother? It makes no difference to him, he's just killing what is in front of him.

So, what if the effects of a person's actions are different from what she intended? We tend to believe that bad things must have a cause. Therefore someone must be to blame and should be punished. Our politicians, who want us to believe that they can make things right, encourage this belief. But actually, it is largely nonsense. Bad things sometimes happen, however diligently we try to avoid them. Punishing failure in order to stop things going wrong only leads to the good honest triers of the world becoming paralysed by fear. Psychopaths, on the other hand, who have no conscience, also fail to learn from experience. So punishment doesn't work either for people who lack the ability to care or for those who care too much. (See Figure 1 for a graphic representation of this.) It really only works for those in the middle. What then is the point of punishment, or even blame? What about conscience and guilt? It seems to me that those who have the most reason to be guilty don't feel guilty at all, and vice versa. Maybe punishing people for the things that go wrong makes the rest of us feel better. Really? Let's bring back public floggings then.

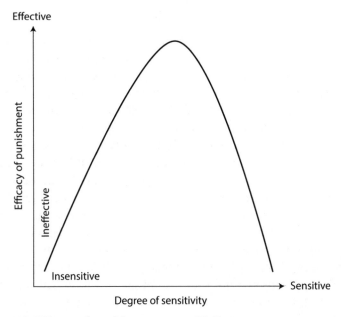

Figure 1 Efficacy of punishment v. sensitivity

The best definition of 'evil' that I have found is: willingness to cause suffering × power. But then I come from a Christian background. I'm aware that many other cultures and religions don't see the infliction of suffering as the premise upon which evil is based. If you're going to punish people proportionally to their degree of evil, we should lock up 90 per cent of politicians and probably knock them around a bit too, for good measure.

If there is no point in punishing mistakes, should deliberate badness be punished? If not, where's the justice? What is justice anyway? Where is the dividing line between justice and revenge? These are difficult questions, the answer to which depends on your perspective. The angry stalker who persecutes his ex-girlfriend feels he is delivering justice for her callous abandonment of him. We tend to feel better if the deliberate infliction of loss or suffering on us or those close to us is met with reciprocal suffering doled out to the perpetrator. The trouble is that revenge is a two-way street. Seeing it as OK means that it is also OK for others to take revenge upon us if they perceive that we have harmed them.

Diversity

Some people are weird, at least from our individual perspective. They aren't normal, by which we mean that they aren't like us, or like we wish to be. But then, as neuroscientists Ronald de Sousa and Douglas Heinrichs pointed out in their 2010 paper 'Will a stroke of neuroscience ever eradicate evil?', if all your ancestors had been normal, you would be a bacterium.

The thing is, the more value judgements you make, the more complicated and disappointing life becomes. When evaluating others, it really isn't in my view worth considering morality. By all means lead what you feel is a moral life yourself. But don't decide how other people 'should' act if you can avoid it. It's too complicated and depends too much on your own perspective. The religiously inspired terrorist believes he is acting righteously, yet the result of his actions is the same as the random brutality of the psychopath, who cares not a jot about right or wrong. The one feels he 'should' carry out his atrocities, the other doesn't understand the meaning of 'should' anyway. It's more effective to understand the person affecting you than to judge him, because then you can best decide what to do about him (in these two examples, you'd best run as fast as you can). Judging how to deal with behaviours works; judging people doesn't. You will see a theme emerging here, and I make no apology for repeating myself. As illustrated in Figure 2, your efficacy in life is increased by strategic thought, but reduced by the amount of time you spend being angry and affronted by people.

So, recognize that everyone is different. In my view, lifemanship (defined in the 1950s by author Stephen Potter, who coined the word, as 'the art of getting away with it without being an absolute plonk') is about charting a course through the sea of different personalities you meet, not expecting them to be like you or to adhere to your values.

$$\text{Your efficacy} = \frac{\text{How strategic you are}}{\text{The number of value judgements you make about people}}$$

Figure 2 Your efficacy

Attitudes

We largely pick up our attitudes in childhood and they tend to persist throughout our lives, though if we're open-minded enough, life can sometimes change us.

Attitudes comprise three components: feelings, beliefs and characteristic behaviours. It's a widely held assumption that we tend to rebel against our parents and their attitudes, but in fact the opposite is usually the case: children tend to mirror their parents as they grow up. We tend to feel the same way about things and to hold the same general beliefs about the world and other people as our parents did, though the evolution of societal norms can change these feelings and beliefs to an extent (for example, there is far less discrimination of all types now than in my parents' day, thank goodness). We may also behave very similarly to the way our parents responded to particular types of situations. We may be ambivalent about some things, but in the end, when push comes to shove, we tend to react to types of people and situations in ways which could have been foreseen before we were born. How disappointingly predictable we are!

Attribution

However understanding we are, and however much we try to avoid making value judgements about people, we all feel about ourselves and those around us based on our attitudes, most of which have been learned in childhood. It would be great if all our attitudes and decisions were logical, but in fact many of them aren't. We tend to misattribute. Attribution is making a judgement according to cause. Let me explain.

Many of us tend to attribute the negative things that happen to others to their thoughts, behaviours or intentions, rather than to external circumstances, whereas we do the opposite with ourselves, in a self-serving way. For example, 'I failed the exam because it was an unfair exam', whereas 'She failed the exam because she didn't study hard enough'. My success is due to merit, but my failure is due to external adverse circumstances, whereas the opposite pertains for you.

In contrast, people who tend to depression do the opposite, undervaluing themselves and their achievements while inflating those of others. Linda, a single mother struggling with three small children, points to one of the other mothers at her kids' school, who works, is active in a charity and is always pretty and well dressed. She ignores the fact that this woman has an army of helpers at work and at home who enable her to look so marvellous. Linda sees herself as plain, talentless and feeble, whereas in fact she does a great job keeping all the balls in the air while she juggles the responsibilities in her life alone.

Most people have a tendency to self-serving attribution, but those who do it least without engaging in self-denigrating attribution (that is, those who are realistic about themselves and others) tend to generate success, while those who do it the most are toxic.

Locus of control

This term refers to whether you control your environment or your environment controls you. Addicts, including alcoholics, typically have an external locus of control, unless and until they get into solid recovery. So, if an alcoholic patient is dried out over a week or so and doesn't engage in any other therapy, I may ask him 'Are you going to stay sober?' Typically he will respond with something along the lines of 'I'll try, but it all depends on my wife. If she keeps on at me, like she does, I'll probably have to have a drink to cope.' Control over his future lies entirely, at least in his mind, with his wife. He'll relapse, probably sooner rather than later, because his locus of control is external to him.

In contrast, someone who has really worked on his recovery, maybe with therapy and help from AA, may respond to the same question with something like this: 'Well, it's going to be tough. My wife and I don't always get along and that could risk my recovery. So I'm going to go to three AA meetings a week, continue my therapy, get a sponsor and phone him for support if I'm feeling at risk.' He's controlling his environment to give himself the best chance of recovery. He has an internal locus of control.

The locus of control is a crucial factor in determining the success or failure of relationships. Relocating the locus of control internally has also been shown to be the single most important change enabled by successful psychotherapy. Believe me, you want those around you to be internally controlled, or you're going to find others depending on you constantly and blaming you when failure happens or anything goes wrong. You need to be internally controlled too, especially if there are toxic people around you, or you will find yourself no more than a tool of their convenience.

Cognitive dissonance

Cognitive dissonance refers to the distance between how things are and how ideally you would like them to be. This may relate to the world, to other people, or in particular to yourself. The cartoon below has already appeared in some of my other books and illustrates this well. The little chap is pumping weights, believing that if he carries on, he will eventually look like Mr Universe, which will make him attractive to women. No it won't. Give it up. You're a scrawny little chap who is more likely to fly to the moon than ever to look like that. If you carry on you'll pull a muscle. But look,

Cognitive dissonance

you're a lovely guy with an engaging personality, a good sense of humour and bags of intelligence. Put down the weights and accept who you are. That is, try to reduce your cognitive dissonance.

Unfortunately, most people's beliefs, as I've explained, tend to be persistent. So we tend not to accept reality even when it's staring us in the face. Instead, we deal with cognitive dissonance essentially by removing dissonant cognitions (our little man refuses to listen to people who warn him that he'll injure himself weightlifting). Or we trivialize or minimize them (Bill tells me to stop working out, but who is he to talk? He's hardly a fine specimen of manhood himself). Or we add a third cognition in order to neutralize them (all bodybuilders take years of pain and injury to achieve their goals; I'll get there in the end).

This explains how toxic people live with themselves. I often hear people saying things like, 'How can he be like that? He's such a horrible bully. How can he live with himself?' The answer is, he uses one of these manoeuvres to persuade himself that what he does is OK. Very few horrible people think that they are horrible (although there are exceptions – see 'Narcissists' on page 50). If a person never accepts criticism and habitually attacks its author, he's probably toxic. Beware.

This also gives us a clue as to how we may start to change the behaviour of a toxic person, by trying to increase his or her cognitive dissonance: be strategic, not angry.

Alternatively, we can work on reducing our own dissonance with neutralizing thoughts (it's not so bad, my boss is a twit but the pay is good). More on this in Chapter 9.

Meaning

The psychotherapist Victor Frankl was a survivor of the Nazis' extermination camps. In his wonderful book *Man's Search for Meaning* (see 'Further reading' for details of all the books I mention), he points out that what distinguished the people who survived, both physically and emotionally, from those who succumbed in that ultimately toxic environment was successfully finding a meaning in their experience and suffering. He subsequently developed a form of psychotherapy (known as 'logotherapy') based on the premise that finding a meaning in one's life is essential for health and well-being.

There's no point in searching for happiness, says Frankl, as it tends to come and go, but if people can develop a real meaning to their existence, they will be likely to chart a course through the toxic waters of life without going under. I'm sure he is right, though I would add that the meaning you find needs to involve choice, not just servitude to those who demand your obedience. Helen's mother (in the Introduction) is the main meaning of her life, but not through choice. Avoiding her mother's displeasure is the real meaning of her existence, though she wishes it wasn't so. She is without choice, her mother's slave.

Projection

This is a mental mechanism present in some more than others, and is a way of dealing with internal conflict. It means taking the aspect of yourself which you find shameful or intolerable, attributing it to others and then attacking it. So, some aggressively homophobic people are confused about their own sexuality and find that this confusion conflicts with their own sense that gender should be unambiguous and people should be 'normal'. By attacking the sexual identity of others, they feel better about themselves. Racists deal with their feelings of inferiority by asserting that their race is better than others, misogynists by denigrating women, religious extremists by hating those of other faiths, and so on. There is a fair chance that the person blaming you feels guilty and inadequate. If so, that person is projecting her self-hatred on to you as a way of feeling better about herself.

At its extreme, projection becomes paranoia, the persecutory delusions of a person suffering from psychosis. But it's more common to witness someone who is angry, red in the face, fists clenched, exclaiming 'Why are you so hostile towards me?' This is difficult to deal with and sometimes quite scary, as it's hard to communicate with someone who is attacking you when you don't know how or why you triggered their anger (see 'Resonance' above).

So these are some of the factors which influence how a person behaves. Next we need to look at groups.

2

Groups and families

'Insanity in individuals is something rare, but in groups, parties, nations and epochs, it is the rule'

Friedrich Nietzsche

Understanding individual people is one thing, but when people come together, group dynamics take over. People can be very different one to one from how they are in groups, and also different in groups of differing types and sizes. So this chapter is about what influences group behaviour, the way individuals behave in groups and in the group from which a child emerges, the family. I have already touched on how parents and early behaviour influence an individual's personality and I will expand on that issue here.

People in groups

Even if you are good at relating to people one to one, groups are another thing completely. Understanding group dynamics helps greatly in coping with them.

Most of us have empathy for the feelings of others and an ability to form and maintain relationships, to a greater or lesser extent, though only if we have had at least some experiences in childhood which teach us how to do so. If all you have experienced growing up is unpredictable violence, cruelty, selfishness and exploitation, it is unlikely that as an adult you will be able truly to feel for others. Most of us have had childhoods which were less than perfect and it apparently does us little harm, but you do need to experience some love, boundaries, moral instruction and affirmation to be able to cope successfully with social demands as an adult.

There is strong evidence that the balance of positive and negative social experiences we have in childhood sets the level of firing of particular nerve fibres in our brains for ever more. These make up what is called the *hypothalamic–pituitary axis* (HPA for short) and the *limbic system*. The HPA is essentially a thermostat which sets our emotional level; the limbic system controls, among other things, our mood, blowing like a fuse when it is overwhelmed. Adverse childhood experiences turn up the HPA, making us tend to overreact to adverse social experiences throughout life, and to reduce the resilience of the limbic fuse. Parents sometimes have a lot to answer for.

For those of us who had less messy childhoods, our behaviour in groups tends to be fairly predictable. In large groups, people tend to rely on others. The more members there are in a tug-of-war team, the less hard each member of the team pulls. On the other hand, approbation improves us. Cheering improves the performance of sports teams.

If a group works collaboratively, that is with everyone participating, it can do better than any individual in tasks involving decision-making. The 'Desert Survival Test', much loved by management trainers, involves a scenario in which your group are the only survivors in a plane crash in a remote desert. You have to decide which items to rescue from the burning plane before it explodes, and in what order. You answer first individually and then, following discussion, as a group. Your answers are compared with those of a survival expert. The exercise invariably shows that the group, working together, provides better answers than any of its constituent members individually.

Being in a group, however, tends to make opinions and decisions more extreme. A group will tend to make riskier (or bolder, depending on your point of view) decisions than an individual, particularly when the members of the group don't know each other. But individuals tend to change their behaviours and beliefs to fit in with the majority. In effect, this often means fitting in with the group member with the most powerful personality (though, as I shall point out, it doesn't have to).

People tend to follow authority. In a study conducted at Yale University in the 1960s, subjects were invited to give electric shocks to 'victims' on the instruction of a professor in a white coat with a clipboard. The subjects were unaware that the victims were in fact actors and the device administering the 'shocks' was a dummy. Two-thirds of subjects continued on command to administer shocks of up to 450 volts, a level indicated on the machine as beyond 'danger' and marked 'XXX', despite their victims showing increasing distress and eventually falling unconscious. Men and women were equally compliant.

Interestingly, the subjects' obedience fell to below half the previous level in a less prestigious building and to below a quarter when the professor was in another room, or when the person in the white coat was not a professor but an ordinary person. If subjects witnessed another subject refusing to give shocks, their compliance fell by a fifth, and if they saw two subjects defying the authority figure, by two-thirds.

Would the same results have emerged had the study been performed in the UK? I don't know, but what is clear is that rebels have a crucial role in society. Or as Edmund Burke said: 'All that is necessary for evil to triumph is that good men do nothing.'

In another study, conducted at Stanford University, a group of volunteers were divided into 'prisoners' and 'guards'. Over time, the guards became increasingly brutal towards the prisoners, and more and more ready to humiliate them. Clearly social role drives behaviour (unless something or someone prevents it).

In a summer camp in Oklahoma, a group of 11-year-old boys thrown together for the first time were studied over several weeks. Groups with powerful identity and cohesion formed quickly, especially when common activities such as sporting contests were set up. Competition between groups led to hostility between them, whereas when groups were obliged to work together on tasks, conflict decreased, while cooperation and understanding increased. However, the mere act of splitting the boys into groups led to discrimination. 'My group is better and the boys in it are good, while the other groups are all bad' was the gist of it. Any differences tended to be amplified; that is, each group saw the boys in the other groups as more different from themselves, and were more inclined to compete with them, than before the groups were formed. Boys quickly began to define themselves by their group membership ('I'm good because my group is'). The scarcer resources became, the more conflict between groups emerged.

These phenomena aren't exclusive to young boys. Just look at a crowd of football supporters. And have a think about recent history with reference to these insights into how groups behave. I have wondered for some time why the residents of South Carolina seem so much friendlier than those of Surrey, where I lived before. I think it is because South Carolina is roughly the same size as England, but has less than 10 per cent of England's population. There is much less competition for space. Introduce a group of rats into a space the size of a house and they will cooperate for food. Put them into a cramped box and they will eat each other.

Anarchic and cruel behaviour on the part of groups isn't inevitable, but it is common. Many people do have altruism and empathy. These are programmed into us as sociobiological drives necessary to keep the genetic line going. But in order for altruism to prevail, we have to resist the temptation to label and to ignore or devalue those who we don't see as being like us.

Prejudice and stigma

We are a tribal species. We have an innate tendency to group ourselves into 'us' and 'them', as we saw above. Thus, unless we make a conscious decision not to be so, we are all prejudiced. That is, we judge people less favourably if they aren't of our group.

The main way in which prejudice can be reduced is through contact. People who mix regularly find it hard to retain their negative judgements about others, but even then only under certain conditions. There has to be equal status (not a relationship like that of servant and master), a reason to cooperate, support for this cooperation from authority and an acceptance from both groups that inter-group friendships are OK. How often are all these conditions met? Not often, which is why prejudice thrives.

Societies and the individuals within them find it easier to assert their worth by comparing others unfavourably to their group. They tend to stigmatize others in order to feel better about themselves. The word 'stigma' comes from ancient Greek, meaning literally the mark placed on a slave to indicate his ownership, subservience and inferiority. So stigma involves recognizing others as different and therefore as devalued. Once the status of 'other' has been attributed, fear kicks in. If we don't understand someone, we may fear that person and assume malign intent. We therefore exclude such people, avoid them, withhold help and try to control them. If they're lucky, we bestow benevolence, we patronize, not as equals but in order to maintain control.

Prejudice and stigma are everywhere. In my experience, many people hold their prejudices very dear. If you try to separate a man from his prejudices, he will try to hurt you. You're going to meet it whoever you are and unless you are very determined and vigilant, you're going to practise it. That's discrimination. It's who we are, unless we aren't.

Scapegoating

The scapegoat also first appeared in the literature of ancient Greece. When crops failed or plague struck, it was assumed that the gods were angry with the people because of their wrongdoings. The convenient solution was to heap all of the community's guilt on to an unfortunate goat, which was then driven out into the desert to starve, thus placating the gods and allowing everyone to feel better. The idea caught on and has been one of the principal ways people have coped with misfortune throughout the ages, as any historian will tell you.

I see a lot of it in dysfunctional families too. The scapegoat, who often has a mental illness or an addiction, is blamed for all the family's woes. 'It's not us, it's him and his addiction. If it wasn't for him we'd all be fine,' is the refrain. So the other members of the family are able to hide their problems and deficiencies behind the smokescreen of the scapegoat.

It's much easier to blame someone else, another group, religion or race, than to take personal responsibility for your life and your failures. It's remarkably difficult to deal with scapegoating, for the same reasons that prejudice and stigma thrive.

Gameplaying

This is a concept developed by Eric Berne, the author of *Games People Play*, and is the focus of transactional analysis, a form of psychotherapy designed for couples and groups. Read the book if you are interested. It's not long and it's a great read, particularly the second half, which describes the 'games' themselves.

Berne saw relationships of any kind as existing on three different levels, and in two different ways. First, a person in a relationship occupies a position of parent, adult or child. If we're talking about a ten-year-old daughter and her mother there's no problem, assuming both accept their roles as parent and child, but if we're dealing with a married couple, there may be. If, say, Jane likes to be in control and treats her husband Jim like a child, this can work, sort of, if the child-like position of having no responsibility and having decisions made for him suits him. If, however, he wants an adult–adult relationship with mutual respect and shared responsibility and decision making, we have a situation in which conflict is inevitable. So the best relationships between adults are of the adult–adult type, but parent–child relationships can also be stable, if both parties sign up to them. Such an agreement is never spoken, as it sounds bad to accept that 'I like being a child, so I let my wife parent me'. It just happens. Figures 3 and 4 illustrate this dynamic. Both relationships are 'parallel', and therefore potentially stable.

Figure 5 (overleaf) shows the situation where Jim wants an adult–adult relationship but Jane wants to parent him. The relationship is 'crossed', meaning it is unstable. Sparks will fly.

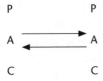

Figure 3 The adult–adult relationship

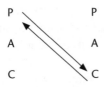

Figure 4 The parent–child relationship

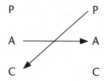

Figure 5 A crossed relationship

The second way in which relationships exist on three levels relates to closeness. The top level is one of spontaneity and intimacy. Spontaneity means you say what you mean when you mean it; you don't store up or repress feelings and issues. Intimacy means emotional closeness. It may also imply physical closeness, depending on the relationship, but it's emotions we're focusing on here.

Spontaneous and intimate relationships are great in the right context, but aren't always appropriate. If, the first time I met you, I started hugging and kissing you, it would probably confirm what you always believed about psychiatrists; we're a very odd lot. It's too spontaneous and intimate for that situation. If, however, on returning home from work, I approached my wife, offered my hand and said, 'Good evening madam, it's a pleasure to meet you,' she would understandably think something was lacking in our marriage. My greeting was one of formality and ritual, which is appropriate on first meeting, but implies too much emotional distance in an established relationship. Formality means an implied emotional distance and ritual means a prescribed set of words and/or actions rendering the interaction predictable and safe, while also implying a lack of hostility and ill intent. The handshake shows you have no dagger in your hand, literally or metaphorically.

There are some relationships, even between husband and wife, which (being parallel) seem to be quite stable on this level, though it's not how I would choose to lead my life. An example is the patient who replied, when I enquired about his marriage:

'It's fine.'

'Oh, but your GP in his referral letter said you and your wife weren't speaking.'

'We aren't.'

'Well, when did you last speak to your wife?'

'Three years ago.'

This man was apparently quite content with the lack of spousal communication, so long as meals were cooked and chores done. What she got out of it who knows. He wasn't keen for me to meet his wife, presumably lest I disturb the stability of their formalized and ritualized relationship.

But what if even a formalized and ritualized relationship breaks down? Maybe the relationship is crossed, or maybe something or someone threatens the status quo. Commonly family, friends or others start to comment on or criticize the relationship. 'I wouldn't let my wife push me around like that, John. What sort of a wimp are you? Stand up for yourself, mate!' Or a whole host of other threats to the status quo of an imperfect relationship.

That's when the lowest level of relationship (see Figure 6) kicks in, which is based on 'gameplaying'.

In this context games aren't a fun pastime, but a covert set of actions designed to put or keep the victim in a position he or she wouldn't voluntarily occupy. Games all have one or more 'payoffs' for the operator, that is rewards which keep them playing the game.

There's an example carried out by Helen's mother in the Introduction. She insists on Helen taking her personally to her hospital appointment despite Helen being overwhelmed with other responsibilities. She can't force her physically, but by reminding Helen of her age and limited life expectancy, she introduces as a penalty for non-compliance a level of guilt which she knows Helen will be unable to tolerate. It's not stated outright, but the implication is 'If you don't do my will, you are a bad daughter and a bad

Figure 6 The three levels of relationship

person.' The payoffs for Helen's mum are power and control over Helen, precedence over Helen's husband and friends in the pecking order, keeping Helen's company without the need to be kind to her in return, and saving money.

One example or variant of gameplaying has been called 'gas-lighting', after the 1944 film *Gaslight*. It is a game often played by people with strong psychopathic or narcissistic traits and involves a consistent attempt to disorientate and confuse the victim in order to bend her to the player's will. Facts, abuse and other events are not only denied, but the memory, sense or sanity of the victim is questioned. Helen's mother reminds her, falsely, that she had promised to take her to the hospital and that Helen had heard the doctor say (which she hadn't) that Mum needed someone to be with her throughout the visit. Over a period of this drip-feeding of false memories, Helen's mother persuades her that her memory and judgement are suspect, so she should just do what her mother says.

Most relationships involve occasional gameplaying. Anyone with a modicum of wit and intelligence has a tendency to manipulate a bit when fearful, tired or unhappy. That's not a problem if there are spontaneity, intimacy, kindness and giving at other times. But when a whole relationship is based on gameplaying or it is a person's go-to form of interaction with others, harm ensues. That is, unless an 'antithesis' is found, a manoeuvre designed by the intended victim of the game which prevents the player from gaining the payoff. More on antitheses in Chapter 10.

Learned helplessness

Helen's childhood looked good from the outside. Her parents provided her with a comfortable house and a good education; they fed her and clothed her well. They were prominent in their community and everyone admired them. They forgot just one thing, which was to teach Helen that she was valued. In truth, they largely ignored her as they were too busy being important. She was able to get away with being naughty as her parents' attention was elsewhere, but by the same token her achievements weren't noticed either. Sometimes her parents would irritably chastise her when she had done nothing wrong, while at other times misdemeanours went unremarked. Over time she learnt that 'It doesn't matter what I do, it doesn't make any difference. Good or bad things may happen to me, but I can't do anything to change them. I have no influence on the world.'

There are two ways this can go. Helen can choose a field of endeavour, say pleasing people, and become so adept at it that she fills a role in her world and that of people around her. That becomes the pattern and meaning of her life. Or she can give up and become a passive recipient of people's whims and injunctions. Either way, she becomes very vulnerable to being used and abused by others.

Teaching someone to be passive is called 'learned helplessness'. It's difficult to induce such a state in a healthy adult who previously was effective and independent, but it can be done. Torturers in dictatorships around the world are taught how to achieve it. They do so by sometimes randomly torturing their prisoners and at other times, equally randomly, feeding them and treating them well. Over time the victim learns, 'It doesn't matter what I do, I can't change anything. I have no power.' It's not easy to achieve; it takes torture or prolonged abuse in someone who previously felt effective. But in a child it's easy. All you have to do as a parent (or to a lesser extent as a teacher) is to fail to teach the child the rules of cause and effect; that she can influence the world around her; that what she does makes a difference.

Attachment and abandonment

From the first days of life we form attachments to other people. The first and most important is to our mothers. Fathers become important too, a bit later on. If your parents do a good job, you learn that your attachment to them is secure. They will always be there and, even if you are chastised for wrongdoing, they will always love you. This attachment forms the basis for all the attachments, including friendships, romance, marriage and parenthood, which form throughout life.

Parents don't have to be perfect, in fact it's better if they aren't. A famous study carried out on the Isle of Wight, where I was born and bred (I wasn't one of the subjects), followed up every child born there over a one-year period, right the way through to adulthood. It worked because many people born there never leave. What the researchers were looking at was which factors had the greatest influence on whether a child grew up emotionally healthy or not. They found, not surprisingly, that the most important factor was the mother, though fathers were also quite important. What was more surprising was that it wasn't the perfect mothers whose children grew up to be most emotionally healthy. These mothers were always there, always loving, never irritable and never left their kids in front of the TV; perfect. The trouble is that the real world isn't like that and these kids grew up struggling with adversity, loneliness and the unkindness of others. Not surprisingly, the children of mothers who were neglectful, abusive, inconsistent or addicted also did badly. But the kids who did best were those born to mothers who were 'good enough'. That is, they were usually warm, loving, consistent and attentive, but they faltered every now and then. They occasionally put the kids in front of the TV when they were tired. They were occasionally snappy, but when they were they subsequently admitted it to their child. The kids learnt the difference between Mum being snappy because she's tired and being cross because I've done something wrong, and they always knew they were loved and it would be OK in the end. So you don't need to be a perfect parent, just to be good enough.

So, what of those children whose parents are absent, abusive, unreliable or drunk? The answer is that their children fail to form a secure attachment, not just to their parents, but also to other people they meet throughout life. Their attachments are insecure, anxious and needy. Such people tend to have unsuccessful relationships for a number of reasons, which is such a shame, because a stable relationship is what they need more than anything. They may be too anxious and clingy, or they may be 'people-pleasers' who attract the users and abusers of the world. They may appear narcissistic, showing off too much to hide their lack of self-worth. Narcissists don't love themselves, they hate themselves. Their selfish boastfulness is a desperate and ultimately doomed attempt to get the world to love them. They may become emotionally extreme and volatile because of an overwhelming fear of abandonment.

Whichever way it goes, these children tend to grow up having problems making and maintaining healthy relationships. As often as not, they tend to find each other as adults and one or both partners tend to be toxic to the other.

Boundaries

Another issue which gets taught in a successful childhood is the setting and respecting of boundaries. This means learning about choice. Small children are entirely self-centred. That's as it should be, as there's time in adolescence to learn that other people matter and that to get what you want you have to obey rules, to be strategic, thoughtful and considerate. You can't just demand that everything go your way. You have to observe limits. But if this isn't taught, or if the child fails to learn from experience, he will become like a bull in a china shop, crashing through the limits, feelings and needs of others and failing to respect their choices, or even to allow them choices at all. Such people, who don't recognize boundaries, have often had disrupted childhoods, particularly around early adolescence. They haven't learnt that others really matter, other than as tools to help them get what they want.

OKness

If you are lucky enough to emerge from childhood having a solid sense of who you are, that's a good start. We don't all ever get this far, some people being fairly confused about their feelings, aims and preferences. This sense of 'I am', as distinct from what is going on around you, is what we call *ego*. Someone with a weak ego is a cork on the ocean, up when good things happen, down when the going gets rough, but with no stable sense of self.

Even better than getting a solid sense of 'I am', is coming to the conclusion that 'I am OK'. This usually comes from good childhood experiences (though good experiences later in life can undo a lot of early damage) and is extremely protective through the ups and downs of life. During my career, I was aware that I wasn't the best psychiatrist in the world. I trained with some of them; highly intelligent, knowledgeable, insightful, charming and intuitive. They also had gorgeous wives and kids and in between being great psychiatrists and publishing seminal research papers, managed to achieve a golf handicap of one. While such people sometimes stirred in me unworthy feelings of envy, I was able to cope with those feelings, because I knew that I was pretty good at my job. I may not have been the best, but I was a long way from being the worst. I was OK. This knowledge allowed me to get on with my job without being unduly influenced by the reactions towards me of my patients and their families. Don't get me wrong, I like being praised and dislike criticism as much as the next man, but I'm not reliant on the one, nor afraid of the other. I'm free to be and do what I choose, not what is going to attract the most praise.

People with OKness are easier to be around than those without it, because what they say is what they mean, not what they think you want them to say, or what will make you admire them. What you see is what you get.

Families

I've already said quite a lot about how your family of origin makes you who you are, and I'm not going to expand any more on the subject here. I will just say this. I have seen many patients who continue to make themselves ill in the belief that 'If I can just do enough for them/be successful/pretty/rich enough, my mum/dad will tell me they love me'. No they won't, and here's why. If by the time you're 40 they haven't told you they love you yet, it's not you, it's them. They won't express their love because they can't. They're emotionally disabled. It is what it is and it won't change.

You may feel I'm too harsh, but I believe that genetics isn't everything. To me a mother is someone who is motherly, a father someone who is fatherly and so on, regardless of their genes. And as it happens, I would add the following. A friend is someone who is friendly. Are all of yours?

That's most of the theoretical background we need to understand to be able to deal with toxicity. But before we go further we need to think about how people can be influenced.

3

Influencing people

Before we go on to look at the sort of people and places who, or which, can harm you, let's do one more thing, which is to consider how people can be influenced. This allows us to understand how people shape their environment, for good or ill, explaining how groups and places become healthy or toxic. It will suggest how we can become better at dealing with others, and also how we can change the way people around us behave in a direction which is healthy for us.

A sociologist friend to whom I showed a draft of this chapter said it looked as if I was trying to teach people how to manipulate others. I'm not, because manipulation is about pushing someone to do something she doesn't want to do, whereas what I'm after is ways of changing your thinking and that of others so that they come together more productively.

Observation

Before you can decide how to cope with people, individually or in groups, you need to observe them. This sounds obvious, but many of the people I see who are suffering from stress-related illness never give a thought to understanding the people who are making them ill. They are too busy trying to please, placate or impress them. Being a real observer means stepping back a bit, saying and doing less, and really watching and listening. This is an aspect of mindfulness, of which more in Chapter 10. You may assume that being quiet and apparently passive in this way would make you unpopular, but in my experience, it doesn't. On the contrary, people tend to like being listened to and being given space to hold the floor.

Understanding

It's important to understand where a person or group is coming from, their perspective and motivations, before reacting to them. If someone says or does something hurtful to you, it may be deliberate or not. He may be acting quite reasonably by his own standards. What he is saying or doing may not be hurtful if said or done to him.

There are at least four filters in a discourse, each of which can lead to misunderstanding. What he said may not be what he meant. What she heard may not be what he said. What she understood may not be what she heard. What she subsequently remembers may not be what she originally understood.

So, a starting point in dealing with people better is to realize that you may not understand them and that they may not understand you. If something is going wrong in an interaction with a person or group, be puzzled, not judgemental, at least until you really understand what is happening for them and for you. *Don't just do something, sit there.*

Understanding is the first priority. Action comes later.

Leadership

Groups seem to thrive under good leadership which brings out the best in its members – that is, all the rest of us. But what is a good leader? Well, it depends on what you're after. Is it to have someone tell you what to do? Do you want a cohesive group? Is it motivation you're looking for? Do you want someone with vision and ideas, or someone good at getting things done? All of the above? OK, then you need Stalin. No, you want someone who listens and takes on board your thoughts and ideas? How about everyone else's ideas, though, if they are incompatible with yours? How is your leader ever going to make a decision?

The truth is that different types of leaders are best in different situations, though some leaders are useless anywhere. One study found that 60 per cent of all organizations had incompetent leadership, and anyway, without power, persuasiveness and an effective vision of what is needed, nobody will succeed as a leader. But, given these qualities, different types of leader are needed depending on the prevailing situation. In very favourable situations, where opportunity abounds and threats are few, a task-focused and directive leader does best. The same is true in very unfavourable situations, where it's a case of battening down the hatches and surviving. But in all other situations, where the organization faces a mix of opportunities and threats, a more encouraging, relationship-orientated leader with strong facilitatory skills does best.

In any case, all leaders need to be accepted by those under them while having the power to make decisions. Not an easy combo, that. Leaders need to foster group cohesion and an effective pursuit of a common goal, while maximizing motivation, minimizing fear and avoiding bullying. Most importantly, they need to be able to set clear, defined goals which everyone can understand, whether or not everyone agrees with those goals.

Communication

Communicating well can get you out of a whole heap of trouble and can change the behaviour of even quite difficult people. It's about being persuasive. What it takes to achieve that depends on several things, though. These include your innate persuasiveness, the type of message you are trying to get across and the characteristics of your audience.

Good communicators are believable and they seem to know what they are talking about. So don't try mouthing off on subjects about which you know nothing. Well-directed questions are much more impressive and persuasive in such situations. Good communicators are likeable (I shall talk later about how to be liked) and they appear to have things in common with their audience. People don't tend to react well to outsiders telling them what's what, or to being talked down to. So if you want to influence people within a group, you need to become an established member of the group first, or at least to persuade them that you're 'one of us'. There is good evidence in addition that physically attractive people are more persuasive. Not a lot you can do about that; you either got it or you ain't. Ever wondered why I stick to the written word? I also have a good face for radio.

To get a message taken on board you need to seem confident without being overconfident. It is a characteristic of failed politicians that they suffer from increasing hubris, which clouds their judgement and eventually brings them down (ex-Foreign Secretary David Owen has written widely on what he terms 'the hubris syndrome').

If several points are to be made to an audience, the first and the last are always remembered better than those in the middle. A moderate amount of humour, for those who are good at it, works well, but should be avoided by those who are bad at jokes. Wry, gently ironic and self-deprecating is often easier to pull off. Saying what you're going to say, then saying it, then saying what you've said is a rule for both journalists and politicians, and it works equally well for the rest of us. That is, stating the main point in more than one way and summarizing it allows your audience to take away something to remember. A clear conclusion is important in any persuasive message, even when the correct action is in doubt. The good communicator is even clear about things being unclear.

If the group you're trying to influence is unsophisticated, giving a one-sided argument works best, whereas if they are educated and well informed, giving both sides of the argument, before explaining why your argument prevails, is more effective.

If the audience is of like mind to the speaker, taking time and speaking slowly achieves the most. If, on the other hand, they hold very different views from those the communicator wants to get across, it is more effective for her to speak quickly. It's most persuasive to start a message not too far from their pre-held beliefs, then to nudge the subject in the desired direction gradually.

Whatever the audience, enthusiasm, conviction, direct eye contact and a relaxed, open stance are all persuasive.

If you have difficulty understanding what all this means in practice, think about how Tony Blair came across. He was the best communicator I've ever seen, whatever you think about his politics. And have a think about how, in 2016, Donald Trump became President of the USA and why Hillary Clinton didn't. It's surprising, isn't it, that some professional communicators seem not to be aware of the basic rules of persuasion I've outlined over the last few paragraphs? In any case, the same rules of communication apply whether you want to influence a group of 2, 60, 60 million or the entire USA.

People who heal

While some people are toxic to some people, others are healing. Research on what makes people who undergo psychotherapy better shows consistently that, in determining whether her patients or clients get better or not, the personal attributes and style of the therapist are more important than the model of therapy she employs. Among the characteristics of such healers are empathy, genuineness, warmth and an ability to listen and reflect in a way which shows that they have heard and understood the issue which has been shared.

This isn't only the case with professional therapists. So many of us, in my experience men particularly, want to fix things. We also want to fix people, so that when distress is shared with us, we want to deliver advice which will make things better. In fact, what is often needed is not solutions, but a sharing of the feelings, for someone to be there and tolerate the sadness without swatting it away with trite advice. Someone who can really listen and stay with a person's distress is immensely healing. Genuine, warm, empathic people make other people better, whether they are trying to or not.

A good example came up when I was starting a research project some years ago, looking at how best to help people to get off Valium. My co-researchers and I were doing the necessary baseline evaluations of our patients, measuring among other things how anxious they were before starting the withdrawal process. This required three meetings with each patient over a four-week period, at each of which a number of rating scales were administered. The researchers were specifically instructed not to deliver any therapy to the patients at these meetings. Nonetheless, we of course chatted generally to them, enquiring casually about what they had been doing, any recent news, the health of their spouses and pets, and such like. To our great surprise, we found that the average level of anxiety among our group of patients more than halved during this run-in period. So much so in fact that they were almost not anxious enough to make the study valid. Warm, supportive communication heals people.

That may seem like a lot of psychology for a book of this sort, but I think that knowing this stuff is crucial, as how to cope with toxic people and places follows logically from it. So now it's time to look at the types of people and places that can make you ill, if you let them.

Part 2
TOXIC PEOPLE AND PLACES

4

Toxic people

I once worked with a man who was truly toxic. Not just to me, though I admit he affected me for a while, but to pretty much everyone he spent any time with. He never missed an opportunity to manipulate a situation to his advantage. He was critical of everyone, undermining, dishonest and untrustworthy. If ever challenged about his behaviour, he would become very threatening. His colleagues lived in fear of him and as far as I know, he made no close professional relationships. How his patients fared I have no idea. Nowadays I suspect that the General Medical Council (the doctors' regulatory body) would have taken a close interest in him. I'll call him Alex, though that wasn't his real name.

When I look back at Alex, two things strike me. The first is that, in his mid-forties, he was occupying a junior post. This must have offended against his need for importance. He certainly wasn't stupid, which suggests to me that being as obviously toxic as Alex limits a person's efficacy and ability to succeed. The second realization I have come to is that, to the best of my knowledge, none of his colleagues really suffered any permanent harm from him. We were fearful of him, he threatened a great deal, but we all emerged largely unscathed. How come?

The answer, I believe, is that he was too obvious. Without donning a pair of horns and a tail and holding a three-pronged pitchfork, he couldn't have been more clearly toxic, which allowed us all to treat him with caution, to give him a wide berth and to treat his pronouncements with appropriate scepticism.

Alex gives us a clue as to how to cope with toxicity.

It would have taken a person with particular vulnerabilities to be damaged by Alex. Someone who, for reasons of their personality or background, was unable to see the threat he posed them or to avoid being influenced by him. I fear that he probably recruited such victims, as he would have been good at finding people to use and abuse, and I fear for their welfare.

The point that Alex illustrates is that very few people are toxic to everybody they come into contact with, or in every situation. There are a few people around who are charming, intelligent, successful – and toxic. Their superior abilities hide their true natures and intentions. These people have an enormous capacity to harm those around them, but fortunately they are rare outside the environs of the Palace of Westminster.

Equally, if you are unfortunate enough to find yourself blocking the path of a psychopath in a dark alley, you are extremely unlucky. Violent psychopathic attacks don't happen very often. A lot more prevalent are individuals who are toxic to some people, or in some situations but not others, or who are toxic only some of the time. This is real life. Most people, unlike Alex, aren't caricatures. In order to prevent ourselves being harmed by people who are toxic to us, we need to understand our own vulnerabilities as well as recognizing how and in what situations such people may harm us. If we don't, we will suffer unhappiness and in due course probably stress-induced illness.

Those most at risk from toxic people are the good, honest givers of the world. Many of the individuals described in this chapter have very sharp antennae and are very good at finding people of this sort, so if you or someone you care about is a giver, you need to pay particular attention to this chapter. Recognition is over half of the battle.

So are you, or is someone you care about, at risk from toxic people? Here's a checklist of vulnerability traits to help you decide. Are you:

- kind
- caring
- trusting
- generous
- forgiving
- liable to put yourself last
- sensitive
- unassertive

- self-critical
- lacking confidence
- keen for approval
- keen to avoid conflict
- anxious
- prone to depression?

If you can answer 'yes' to more than half of the above, you may be vulnerable to toxic people.

What follows is a set of descriptions of some of the personality types who have proved toxic to my patients. It's worth developing the ability to recognize these traits and behaviours, though in life you will find that people rarely fall neatly into one category or another, more often exhibiting a mixture of different traits and behaviours at different times or in different situations.

Once more I want to emphasize that I'm making no moral judgement about people with these traits. I'm not saying that they are lacking worth or reprehensible in any way. Many will be struggling through life with the legacy of a childhood dominated by loss, chaos or abuse. The point is that if you recognize and have a way of dealing with people who have the capacity to be toxic specifically for you, you will be healthier and happier.

The sexes of my examples are alternated. This does not imply that these traits are more common in one sex or the other.

Boundary invaders

George is known as a fixer, a salesman. He gets what he wants. He can always get a table at a full restaurant at the last minute without a reservation and is given a discount in a shop when there is no sale on. He arrives at a 'black tie' event in jeans and a T-shirt and nobody turns a hair. 'Oh, that's just George, he's unique.' People admire his audacity and marvel at how much he gets away with. His antics can be amusing, and his ability to breeze in and take charge in situations the rest of us find intimidating can be reassuring when your aims and his coincide.

George pushes and challenges any limits put in his path. It's how he operates, and he's found that it works very well for him. He despises people who conform to accepted norms and sees life as a struggle in which only those who dare win. He's a good guy to have on your side.

But there's the kicker. He isn't on your side, not really. He's out for himself, and sooner or later that isn't going to be good for you. He'll ask you for things, to do things for him or for a loan. He won't repay what you lend him and when, some weeks later, you ask when he's going to pay you back, he is affronted, leaving you feeling as if you've stepped over the line and insulted him. If you don't challenge him, the demands on you only grow. The boundary between what is and isn't acceptable is shifted slowly and subtly, so that challenging any one example would seem petty and mean. Eventually you become exhausted and have to say 'no' to his latest demand. Given that the norm was you saying 'yes', he feels entitled to take offence and he stomps off in high dudgeon. If you aren't assertive enough to refuse his demand, you may tell a little lie to excuse yourself. 'I would have run the errand for you, George, but I have to baby-sit for a friend this evening.' He will move heaven and earth to uncover your deception. 'Which friend? What's their phone number? I'll phone them; I'm sure they'll see that my need is greater this evening.' When your deception is uncovered, the misdemeanour is broadcast and logged, to be played back to you the next time you consider resistance.

And so you are enslaved. When, inevitably, you become exhausted and succumb to a stress-related illness, George will blame you for not being there for him and will tell you that 'it's all in your mind'.

If George is your parent, he will remind you frequently of the debt you owe him for bringing you up and indeed for life itself, omitting the fact that he didn't do much other than to criticize and intimidate you when you were a child. But if you please him well enough even now, maybe, just maybe he will one day say he loves and appreciates you.

Dream on. He never will because it isn't in his make-up. It isn't you, it's him.

At its most subtle, boundary invasion can be difficult to spot. There are clues, though, in language and feelings. Words such as 'just', as in 'I don't need much, just a few minutes of your time' and 'only', as in 'I'm only asking for one little favour' are giveaways. If a person is protesting about how little he is demanding, the chances are that he is asking for more than he should. At the end of the day, if it makes you feel uncomfortable, resentful or unhappy, it may be boundary invasion. It's certainly worth giving it some thought and possibly discussing it with someone else before saying 'yes'.

The thing is that some people who invade boundaries aren't toxic. They're fun. Their audacity is amusing and sometimes useful. Where is the dividing line between audacity and toxicity? As with the other examples in this chapter, the answer isn't easy and depends on their effect on you. If you can set limits with George and he can accept them, you'll be OK, however he behaves towards the rest of the world.

Nuclei of chaos

Mildred arrives in your life like an explosion, grabbing your attention with her vitality and immediacy. She sweeps you off your feet with her ability to blow with the wind, to experience life with extremes of emotion that make you feel really alive. She treats you like the most important person in the world, so special that she can't believe she has found you. You feel somehow more significant, greater in her presence.

The trouble is that you aren't the first and you certainly won't be the last. It's great when the whirlwind which is Mildred settles around you, but soon it will pick you up and dump you on the rubbish heap. Mildred is emotion, that's all there is, and it's extreme. When she's up she's exultant, when she's down she's in the deepest pit imaginable and she takes you along with her. If you do a bit of historical digging you'll find that Mildred has left a trail of destruction in her wake, like a tornado. Everyone was her unique hero, then inevitably in due course a demon to be cast out or punished.

That's if you're lucky. If you're particularly tenacious or for some other reason hang on to Mildred for longer than most, you're in for more trouble. This is because Mildred doesn't just *act* chaotically and dramatically, she *is* chaos and drama. She has no solid identity, preferences or values, just impulses which change by the minute. So if you're in favour one moment and out of it the next, it's not personal, it's just Mildred changing constantly as she does. Because she feels empty, she depends on the world giving her what she wants. So if things go her way she's ecstatic (briefly), but if they go against her, she's plunged into deep despair. She may react to what you felt was a fairly mild disagreement by lashing out at you or by harming herself. She will probably threaten suicide from time to time. I wish I could reassure you that she won't act on her threats, but I can't, because Mildred is above all unpredictable. I've sadly known a number of Mildreds who have, for example, taken a fatal overdose, believing that the tablets they took were harmless because they are available over the counter (paracetamol is one of the most toxic drugs in existence when taken in overdose), or leaving a phone message for their partner saying what they've done, but which is picked up too late. Drama is risky.

Mildred's extreme reactions to you, and to everything and everyone, are just who she is. The cycle of dramas will never stop (unless she seeks effective treatment, in which case it'll take a while). If you're in Mildred's wagon it's going to be a bumpy ride. Better buckle up.

Users, abusers, loafers and energy vampires

Joel is your opposite and you attract him. He fits snugly into the space provided by your trusting, generous and caring nature. He will take anything you give him and leave you feeling that somehow it wasn't enough. He very rarely pays for a drink and it's remarkable how often he forgets his wallet. He's always too busy when you need help, unless the task amuses him. He will emphasize what good friends you are, but you'll be hard pressed to say how he has been a friend to you (remember, the definition of a friend is someone who is friendly towards you). You tend to feel obligated to Joel and yet he feels no reciprocal obligation to you. His sense of entitlement is limitless. You'll often find yourself feeling grateful for the gift of his presence, though you're not sure why. The answer is that, over the years, Joel has perfected the ability to make people feel they owe him (time, effort, money, whatever). This may involve charm, manipulation, humour or any of the other manoeuvres listed elsewhere in this chapter. The bottom line is that he is a taker. He gets what he wants and doesn't care a great deal about what that means for you or anyone else. While Joel may make you feel needed and even loved, don't be fooled. When you are no longer able to give him what he wants he will drop you and move on.

Most Joels are also abusive. Not necessarily physically abusive, though they may be that too, but always abusive emotionally. By this I mean that Joel treats your feelings and welfare with contempt. If he is feeling like it he may be kind and charming, but if he's irritable or upset he'll have no compunction in taking it out on you. He'll do whatever he feels like doing. You'll find yourself worrying about what sort of mood he's in today and trying to behave in a way that will put him in good humour.

A minority of abusers are sexually abusive. People who sexually abuse their own or other people's children are at the extreme end of this category, and display the most pronounced personality traits. This isn't surprising, as sexual abuse of children is a big boundary to cross. For Joel to persuade himself that he should act in this way, he has to employ some fairly powerful psychological strategies.

Joel the child sexual abuser uses whatever is at his disposal to get what he wants. This includes power, as in the high-profile celebrity who uses his fame to gain access to children and persuade them to do what he wants, or the teacher who abuses the authority he holds over his pupils. It also includes denial, rationalization and blaming. 'I didn't do it. It was a misunderstanding; my innocent affection was misinterpreted' or 'It was an aberration caused by stress. I wasn't thinking straight, it will never happen again' (yes it will, unless you acknowledge your responsibility and seek some help), or 'The kid seduced me, egged me on. I was a victim of her sexual precociousness'. All these statements are typical of the sexual abuser. Instead of taking responsibility for his actions, Joel will justify them or attempt to lie his way out of trouble. He deliberately ignores the fact that children aren't responsible; responsibility comes with adulthood. He will use all of his experience and manipulative skills to intimidate and force compliance on his child victim, persuading her that if she blows the whistle, she will be blamed.

Many forms of abuse are more subtle than this and the victims can be of any age. But what all abuse has in common is that the abuser has the power and the victim has none. Joel always wants to have his way and to bend you to his will.

The loafer is also abusive, but in a passive way. Joel the loafer is a user who relies on your conscience, sense of duty and perfectionism to get out of doing anything for himself. He will be a master of self-deprecating humour, which somehow makes his sloth OK, until inevitably you start to become the focus of his barbs. Joel assumes you are there to carry out his wishes and your tendency to put yourself last plays into his hands. He really is a waste of space, but he manages to make you feel that it is a privilege to be allowed to serve him. He slips under the radar, because he is charming, because other people like him, and it is a while before you realize that you are being taken for a ride. By then, you'll feel used up and when Joel finds that you have no more to offer him, he'll cast you aside without so much as a thank you. In fact, it'll probably all be your fault. Don't ask; it's not supposed to make sense, unless you start from the premise that only Joel matters.

Finally, Joel the energy vampire, who is a kind of loafer, but with a suction hose designed to extract the life from you. He finds you because you give of yourself. You are one of those people who is a natural carer, who always tries to make people feel better. He will give you a tale of woe which goes on indefinitely. When you suggest a solution, he sweeps it aside with 'Yes, but I can't do that because . . .' This is also a type of game, as we shall see in the next section. His problems, complaints and worries have no end and if you try to take any of them away, he'll resist you with all his might. At the end of the exchange you're left exhausted and deflated, while Joel seems energized. This is because Joel has managed to transfer his frustration, worry and unhappiness on to you while taking your energy for himself. The truth is that we all feel better if we share some of our sadness and worry: 'a problem shared is a problem halved'. Joel takes this principle and doesn't stop until you are sucked dry.

If you find yourself often being called upon to listen to a person's problems, only to be caught in an interminable cycle of 'Why don't you . . .?', 'Yes, but . . .'; if you frequently find yourself frustrated, despairing, sucked dry by the same person who appears to have forgotten about the problem the next day while you've been mulling it over all night, you may be in the presence of an energy vampire.

Gameplayers and manipulators

I described the phenomenon of gameplaying in Chapter 2. To remind you, it refers to a covert set of actions performed by the player and designed to place you in a position you would not voluntarily occupy. Most of us play games occasionally, when we're not at our best, but for a few people gameplaying is what they do all the time. It's how Mabel gets what she wants, and she's done it all her life. Her mother did it, and her grandmother before her. As a child, it kept Mabel under her mother's control, and now it's who she is. Nothing Mabel says can be taken quite at face value; it all has a purpose. Say you and Mabel live together and you are deciding what to do this evening. You want to go out, but Mabel wants to stay in. In a healthy relationship you will talk it through, negotiate, possibly coming to a compromise in which you go out briefly but eat in. But in a gameplaying relationship no real exchange of views takes place.

'Let's go out to eat,' you say.

'OK, but my tummy is playing up again. I think the rich food may not agree with me,' replies Mabel.

'Do you want to stay in then?'

'No, no, I know you don't like staying in with me. You'd rather be with friends. I'll be all right.'

'Are you sure?'

'I don't know, but you want to go out. I'll come out and just spend the evening on the toilet. I'm sure you'll find one of your friends to talk to. You spend so much time with them.'

'Oh, maybe we'd better stay in then.'

'Whatever you like, I'm easy. Just phone up for a pizza, will you?'

Game, set and match to Mabel. She's got her wish to stay in *and* made it your idea. She doesn't have to feel bad about depriving you of your preference, and as a bonus she's made you feel guilty for spending so much time with other people. She's been working on fostering this guilt for some weeks and will use it in due course to ensure that you spend more time in her service uninterrupted by socializing.

There are thousands of such games, but most of them rely for their operation on your guilt and sense of duty. Mabel gets regular payoffs (rewards) for her gameplaying because you react in exactly the way she has designed. There is no spontaneity or real intimacy in your relationship, just subtle control.

Manipulation is closely related to gameplaying and has the same purpose: to bend you to Mabel's will. It relies on specious logic; that is, it seems reasonable though it isn't. So, say Mabel is addicted to opiates (very strong painkillers which can cause a 'high'; heroin and morphine are examples). Mabel arrives at my clinic at 6 p.m. on a Friday evening demanding a prescription for methadone (a heroin substitute). She says I have to give her the prescription because she lost her medication when it fell out of her pocket into the river. Her doctor's surgery is closed and if I don't supply the drug to cover the weekend she'll have a fit and die. Such an inter-action, in almost exactly this form, has happened to me at least a dozen times in my career.

Now, I know that opiate withdrawal isn't fatal; it may be unpleasant but it won't cause a fit or kill you. But many doctors aren't aware of this and so give out the prescription, which ends up being sold on the black market. They've been manipulated by a master. We've all been manipulated at one time or another as we all have our blind spots, but if the same person succeeds in doing it a lot, you have a problem.

If you spend much of your time feeling pushed, constrained, guilty or worried about someone, you may be in the presence of a gameplayer or manipulator.

Bullies and sadists

Clive is a bully. There is really nothing you can do with him, unless you thrive on conflict yourself. As it says in the poem 'Desiderata': 'Avoid aggressive persons, they are vexatious to the spirit'. Clive uses aggression to get his way and he's very good at it, having behaved this way all his life. As a kid his family operated on the principle that cruelty is good, so long as you win. The strongest gets the prize and the rest are losers. There really isn't anything else to Clive; it's all about intimidating those around him in order to dominate them and force them to do what he wants. You can't argue, rationalize or negotiate with him because he isn't motivated by truth, sense or fairness. It's no use appealing to his better nature as he doesn't have one. He won't take no for an answer, so acquiesce, withdraw or dig in for battle; it's going to be long and tough.

If you try to stand up to Clive he'll raise the stakes until you give in; he'll always get his way, or there'll be hell to pay. He may intimidate you with violence or the threat of it, but more often his weapon will be humiliation. He may have a group of hangers-on which he needs so that your humiliation is public. And they need him as he makes them feel strong, part of the alpha group, so it's a symbiotic relationship. He keeps his acolytes in check the same way he does you.

Alternatively, Clive's bullying may take place behind closed doors, with you the only victim. To everyone else and in public he's kind and attentive, the perfect parent, spouse, partner or friend. If he is violent to you and you threaten to leave him, he will be apologetic for a while and promise you that he will change. It won't last though, because his frustration and need to subjugate will eventually become overwhelming. Aggression is who he is.

Let's be clear here: violence and intimidation aren't normal, whatever Clive says. Loving people don't hit, intimidate, humiliate or bully their partners. Not even on a bad day, not even when drunk, not even once.

Clive the sadist is particularly scary. He has all of the characteristics of a bully, but in addition he enjoys your suffering. He really gets off on the distress of others, being primarily motivated by inflicting pain and humiliation. He relishes hurting you in any way that he can, whenever the opportunity arises.

While some sadists are criminal, like the sexual sadists who populate crime novels, most are more subtle. Clive may have fantasies of sadistic sexual practices, but he won't act on them, as he wouldn't like the consequences of getting caught. Instead he uses everyday situations, words, humour, judgements and power to cause you the discomfort and humiliation he so loves to witness. He is charming, but only until he has caught you in his web, when he will abruptly change into a monster. If he has bought you expensive meals or jewellery, such gestures will be short-lived. Soon enough he will start criticizing and humiliating you in public and revealing all of those intimate secrets you confided in him when he seemed to be your friend. When you try to get away, the gifts and apparent generosity he bestowed on you early in your relationship will be thrown at you, making it clear that you're in Clive's debt and won't be allowed to leave until you pay what you owe. If you do leave, he will go to extraordinary lengths to try to reel you back in. The old charm, kindness and generosity will return. But don't be deceived. If Clive has taken pleasure in hurting you before, he'll do so again once he's got you back in range.

A brief aside here. Consensual sadomasochistic sexual practices are not the same as real sadism. The reason is that the relationship is loving and the enactment of sexual fantasy is part of the giving of one partner to the other. The 'dominant' partner isn't really subjugating his 'victim'. He's doing what they have agreed and stops if there's any hint of real distress. Be careful though. Don't get into any sadomasochistic games unless you know your partner really well and trust him or her absolutely.

Bombs and bombasts

Sarah doesn't mean any harm, but she causes a lot of it. She's vivacious and fun, but also fiery and unpredictable. From time to time she explodes, and her temper is as frightening as it is bewildering. You really don't know what will set her off, and sometimes neither does she. She feels out of control, without stability, like a yacht without a keel, and she is. If you're on the receiving end, a better metaphor is that Sarah is a machine gun on a tripod with a broken ratchet. The trigger is pulled and the gun spins around on the tripod. Bullets spew out in all directions. If you happen to be standing in the way of one you'll get hit. It wasn't aimed at you, but you were there, so you got shot.

Sarah is unnerving to be around, as you're waiting for the next explosion and you tend to tread on eggshells when you're around her. But you stick around as Sarah is fun and under the apparent fierceness she's really a nice person. She hurts you a lot though, whether she means to or not.

Sarah the bombast has much the same effect. She's not explosive, but she is out of control. She's a big personality with little restraint, a bull in a china shop. She means well, but she tramples all over your feelings and sensibilities without realizing it. Her insensitivity takes your breath away. When Sarah humiliates you in public it is through thoughtlessness, not design, but the effect on you is the same. The weakness or peculiarity you are so ashamed of is broadcast because Sarah didn't realize you were sensitive about it (though you have told her several times). She is being consistent here, as Sarah isn't ashamed about anything. She just barrels through life without an apparent thought for the wreckage left in her wake.

Bigots, blowhards, fundamentalists and zealots

Donald is so obviously toxic that he almost isn't toxic at all. His certainty that anyone of a different race, religion, sex, sexual orientation or football supporters' club from him is inferior is ridiculous. For this reason it's easy to become complacent and believe that he is a harmless eccentric who poses you no threat. If you belong to his tribe in every regard he doesn't immediately threaten you, but he will. Nobody is exactly the same as their neighbour, and unless you too are a bigot and are prepared to agree with every half-baked pronouncement Donald utters, the chances are that he'll turn on you in the end. His prejudice isn't open to argument and so when he turns against you, there is no point in discussion or negotiation. Prejudice is just prejudice and ever more shall be so. In any case, Donald has low self-esteem, though he'd never admit to it. His bigoted assumption that his Caucasian Christian straight male membership of the Bigtown United Supporters' Club makes him special is all he's got. He has to prove he's better than you, or he'll have to confront his underlying belief that he is inadequate. This is why Donald guards his prejudices so fiercely.

Blowhards are certain they know best, and they broadcast the fact loudly. If you disagree with them you will face their wrath. They tend to find their way on to committees, which they dominate with their ill-thought-out ideas. They are full of their own importance and their pomposity gets in the way of any sensible, agreed compromise to which everyone else has signed up. They really are a pest and can be worse than that if the task at hand is urgent.

Fundamentalists are also certain. Their literal interpretation of whatever text they adhere to brooks no discussion or argument. This may apply to religion or to a thousand other issues, big or small. Donald knows all the rules, and if he believes that the hedge separating your properties is a centimetre too high, or your car parked a foot too near his drive, he will not sleep until he has unearthed an ordinance from 1328 proving that you are in the wrong. So cut your hedge or move your car, but unfortunately it won't stop there. Donald will continue to harry you on one pretext or another until you stop answering your door and your mail, or you move.

Zealots are fundamentalists with limitless energy. Donald the zealot will pursue his certainty, if necessary unto his or your death. Don't get in his way, because he will bring you down. If you get into a legal dispute with him he will continue to appeal until you, he or both of you are bankrupted. If you refuse to buy into his belief system he will see it as his duty to destroy you, metaphorically, emotionally or literally.

Fundamentalists and zealots are obviously dangerous people. In fact, I would suggest that anyone who is absolutely certain of anything should be treated with caution.

Narcissists

Elizabeth likes to be liked. No, she has to be liked. It isn't because she is in love with herself; on the contrary she hates herself. Being liked, loved, admired feels like a matter of life and death to her, and it really is that important to her ego (see Chapter 2). What, narcissists aren't in love with themselves? Well no, not usually. In contrast to Narcissus, the character from Greek mythology who fell in love with his reflection, Elizabeth has always seen herself as having no intrinsic worth. As a child her parents never made her feel worthwhile or important just for being her. In order to compensate for this she tended to be the class show-off at school, always having stories that showed her to be one better than her peers. Her house was bigger, her parents more important, her toys more expensive and so on. Not surprisingly this made Elizabeth fairly unpopular at school. The more she was rejected, the more desperate became her efforts to wring out the acceptance and admiration she craved from anyone she could get to listen. In the end she became a very sad and isolated child.

By the time Elizabeth reached adulthood she had a gaping hole the size of a beach ball where her ego should be. Now she's your work colleague and her need for affirmation is desperate. This makes her a difficult person to work with: everything has to be her idea, she always has to be right and she must always be better than you. She certainly isn't a team player, and though you try to like her, she makes this very difficult as she just will not reciprocate and give you anything, though she does hang around you a lot and tells you that you are her best friend.

If you are lacking in confidence yourself, Elizabeth's attention, self-centred though it is, may be welcome, but it comes with unlimited demands. When later you fail to meet these expectations, Elizabeth will be hurt and very likely angry and vindictive. Hell hath no fury like a narcissist scorned.

When I was starting out in psychiatry my psychotherapy trainer told me, 'If you ever meet someone who really, really needs your help, for goodness' sake don't give it to them.' What he meant was that I would be picking up on the unlimited neediness of someone with no intrinsic ego strength. No therapist can fill the gap left by a lack of proper nurturing as a child. If a therapist says to such a patient, 'Don't worry, I'll heal you; I'll always be there for you,' he may think he's telling the truth, but he isn't. And in the end, when he fails to deliver the infinite love, total caring and constant affirmation his client feels he has promised, he will have served only to solidify the harm she has already suffered, by confirming her prediction that everyone will let her down in the end.

So are you prepared for Elizabeth to come home to live with you and to be her constant source of affirmation and reassurance? No? Then start setting limits right now if you don't want to hurt Elizabeth or to get hurt yourself.

Psychopaths/sociopaths

I talked a little about this group in Chapter 1 and I'm fairly sure that Alex, whom I introduced at the start of this chapter, was the real deal. He had the classic characteristics of the psychopath in being entirely lacking in conscience, empathy and the ability to learn from his mistakes, or from sanctions or the opprobrium of others.

As far as I'm aware he never murdered anyone or perpetrated any violent crime, but then intelligent psychopaths are rarely violent. There are fortunately very few Hannibal Lecters in the world. Much more often these people use wit, charm, humour, manipulation and strategy to get what they want. It's easy to be charmed by a psychopath, as he tends to hone these skills effectively through life; you get more by charm than by threats. But let's be clear: if Alex needs to threaten you to get what he wants, he will. He has no real feelings for anyone. Everything he does is designed with an end in mind – and that end doesn't include you, your welfare or your feelings.

How can you recognize Alex for what he is? It isn't easy, as he has spent a lifetime perfecting his camouflage. Psychopaths don't usually have an evil laugh, live in converted volcanoes, own impossibly fluffy cats or profess plans for world domination (James Bond, *Dr No*? Oh, never mind). Over time though, if you are attentive you'll pick up that Alex is all charm and no substance, that he is capricious, totally self-centred, opportunistic, unscrupulous and without real feeling, compassion or humanity. Evaluate a person by his actions, not his words, particularly when the chips are down. If the psychopath in your life is subtler than Alex and better at sucking you in, beware. He may not hurt you physically, but hang around him long enough and when it suits him he will harm you one way or another.

Paranoid possessors

Mary is insecure. That's part of her charm. Her vulnerability is alluring and her reliance on you makes you feel strong and protective. But Mary has a script in her head which she feels sure will always be played out. 'I'm unlovable and even if a guy seems true, he'll eventually get tired of me, cheat on me and then leave me. I'll always be let down in the end.' That's about the size of it. You can reassure her all you like: 'No, I won't let you down, I'll always be faithful.' But 'Uh huh, they all say that, you just wait,' will be the gist of her reply.

Mary starts off being devoted, but over time she becomes increasingly clingy and possessive. She becomes very unhappy if you plan to do anything without her. When you go out to dinner together she starts to accuse you of eyeing up the waitresses. Then she starts checking your emails, texts, bank statements and phone records. Innocent items are flourished accusingly as evidence of your infidelity. In the end Mary inevitably causes her own prediction to come true, as your relationship can't survive the hostility and you break up. Mary's world view is confirmed. She'll always be let down in the end – and unhappy though she is, there's a kind of grim satisfaction in that.

There is a blurred dividing line between this sort of jealous insecurity and the phenomenon of delusional jealousy, but the distinction is crucial. A degree of jealousy is a normal part of a loving relationship, in which both partners have a strong loving attachment to each other. If there's too much jealousy the relationship won't last. But when the distinction between fantasy and reality is lost, things get dangerous. A delusion is a false, fixed belief which is not understandable in terms of the culture of the person concerned (as, for example, a religious belief would be) and is unshakeable by rational argument. Delusional jealousy – that is, the certainty that one's partner is engaged in an affair in the face of overwhelming evidence to the contrary – is among the phenomena in psychiatry most frequently associated with serious violence. Mary angrily brandishes a sheaf of printouts of random bills and emails claiming that they are evidence of your affair and waves a pair of your underpants in your face, pointing out what she says are semen marks and your lover's pubic hair. The more you protest your innocence and give rational explanations for her findings, the angrier Mary gets, until eventually she hits you with a frying pan. Afterwards in A&E she is sorry. She asks for your forgiveness and demands reassurance that it will all be OK. But it isn't OK. Unless Mary gets some effective treatment you are in danger.

There are many shades of possessiveness well short of delusional jealousy, and you aren't at physical risk just because your partner is a touch insecure. But can you discuss her concerns rationally? I'm not saying Mary should always trust you. I think trust is often over-rated, as with the husband whose affair has been discovered and has been forgiven, who then tells his wife: 'This marriage will only work if you trust me.' Why? Trust has to be earned, and once lost takes a long time to re-establish. In the meantime he should welcome as much checking on him as his wife chooses to engage in.

It is when your partner is constantly seeing fictitious evidence in everyday items and events and this takes over your lives that the situation becomes toxic.

Doubters and avoiders

William seems perfect, almost too good to be true. He's good-looking, intelligent, charming, moderately wealthy, and at 38 you're surprised he isn't married. You've established that he isn't gay and your romance is coming along nicely. Given that, at 35, you've just emerged from a divorce after eight unhappy years of marriage, you feel lucky to have found him.

William pursues you with a great deal of romance and persuasiveness. He has his work cut out as you understandably feel 'once bitten, twice shy', and you're not going to be quick in letting your guard down. But William persists and eventually you fall for him. One evening you ask him where he feels the relationship is going and whether he could see you one day moving in together. At that moment, for the first time, you feel William tense up. He starts being evasive, and the atmosphere in the room drops by 20 degrees. Over the next few weeks William doesn't phone and it becomes increasingly difficult to get hold of him. Eventually you become impatient and you ask William if he wants to end the relationship. He says no and for a while everything returns to normal. But just when you think your relationship is back on track, the same thing happens all over again and William once more goes AWOL. You ask mutual friends and it's clear that he isn't seeing anyone else, but his best friend points out that William has always been like this. He's a commitment-phobe.

OK, that's it, life's too short. You phone William and tell him it's over. He's shocked and surprisingly upset. If he cared so much about your relationship, you say, where has he been all this time? He asks you to give him another chance, and reluctantly you do. He's attentive again for quite a while, but this is only the cycle repeating itself and soon enough he does another disappearing act. Now it's really over and you tell William not to contact you any more. But he does, several times a day. Gifts of flowers and jewellery start arriving, he tries to persuade you to come away with him on a holiday to the Maldives and when that doesn't work, out of the blue, he proposes marriage.

Any idea what will happen if you accept William's proposal? Spot on – right first time. It will be a long and lonely engagement which will last until the day one or other of you dies, unless you really leave him. And that won't be easy, because William will move heaven and earth to get you back if and when you make any attempt to do so.

This cycle will go on for ever unless you stop it, because doubting is what William is. Whatever he has he is compelled to escape from. Whatever he doesn't have he is compelled to acquire. There is no end. When you aren't around, William idealizes you. When you are around, he is tormented by the uncertainty over whether you are 'the one' or whether there may be someone even better out there.

I tell you, if I had a hot dinner for every 45-year-old I've seen who has given 20 years of his or her life to an obsessional doubter, I'd be morbidly obese. It's doomed. Accept that and maybe there's a life for you even now. That is, unless William accepts treatment and sticks with it . . .

William the phobic avoider, on the other hand, will recruit you into his world of avoidance. If, say, he's phobic about dirt and contamination, he'll have you washing your hands, cleaning the counter-tops, removing your shoes, boiling clothes, double-cleaning the crockery and cutlery and more, until your whole day is filled with these activities. He may also insist that you copy his meaningless rituals (such as, for example, always doing things in threes), because of the magical thinking which is an element of his obsessive-compulsive disorder (OCD). He fears that if his rituals aren't carried out, something bad will happen. The trouble is that William's OCD is likely to expand over time, unless he seeks treatment, and even if you can cope with it now, in due course it is likely to become unmanageable. If William has always tended to be this way and you can see that his behaviours have remained stable over time – a harmless quirk if you like – fair enough. But if you find that his illogical demands on you are escalating, that's a problem which is going to require action.

Scorekeepers

Izzy is your best friend. At least she says she is. She certainly does a lot for you and is generous to a fault. But then she starts pointing out that your friendship is one-sided. You don't give Izzy as much as she gives you. It would be difficult to do so, as you have other friends and if you attended to all of them as much as Izzy attends to you, you'd never sleep. So you always feel in Izzy's debt, and she's not slow to remind you of the fact.

Izzy uses giving as a weapon. She has a deep sense of injustice. She's given everything, but does she ever get back so much as a thank you? Does she heck. This is her life script and she's constantly looking for evidence to back it up. Her gifts and service are over the top and if you don't reciprocate in kind you'll face her opprobrium, because she's keeping score. Very tiring and stultifying – and difficult to see coming or to extricate yourself from, as Izzy seems so kind. It seems mean to say no to someone who gives so much. So you're enslaved.

Jokers and storytellers

Bill is a funny guy. He's a walking joke book, a master at teasing, ribbing and practical jokes. The thing is, though, he's a bit cruel. His jokes at your expense tend to get people laughing at you, not with you. You have to laugh along with Bill, however unkind his humour is, or you'll be labelled as having no sense of humour. Bill, along with all comedians, knows that if you want to make a statement and not have it challenged, you should make it a 'joke'. 'Oh, stop taking it so seriously, I was only joking' can smuggle the most offensive comments past the censor. There is an honourable tradition, going back to Shakespeare's fools and beyond, of humour being used to say the otherwise unsayable.

The thing is, I think a joke is only funny if everyone present enjoys it, or at least if nobody present is hurt by it. This doesn't mean you can't use humour to prick the balloons of pompous windbags, but preferably not when they are in the room. Politicians, celebrities and confident peers are fair game, as they are able to give as good as they get or are in positions of power and privilege, but Bill prefers to pick on more vulnerable people who don't have the confidence or wit effectively to fight back. Humiliation isn't funny, at least not to me. People who regularly use their humour to inflict suffering and gain control in a group setting are in my view bullies in disguise and among the most toxic of people.

Bill is also a gossip. He tells all sorts of stories about people, most carrying a little grain of truth but magnified by his skilful use of hyperbole. The purpose is the same as that of his jokes: to gain control, subjugate dissent and foster popularity. Gossiping can be harmless fun, but only if nobody gets hurt. Before spreading an item of gossip it's always worth considering what effect it will have on the person or people it concerns when, inevitably, it gets back to them. The chances are that Bill made it up or embellished it. Given his established cruelty, do you really want Bill's version of reality to prevail? Unfortunately it often does, as he's very believable and an engaging storyteller.

Addicts

Sally often tells people she loves them, but only when she's drunk. It's not worth taking much notice of this, or of anything else she says when under the influence, as she won't remember it in the morning anyway. In truth Sally doesn't love you, or anyone else for that matter. Whatever her drug or behaviour of addiction, all Sally really cares about is how to get her next hit. It makes no difference if she is an alcoholic or a drug addict, or is addicted to gambling, food, dieting, exercise or sex (addiction is any set of behaviours which are performed to avoid feelings, and which over time get out of control). Sally may have been the most wonderful and caring friend, mother, partner or wife before her addiction took hold, but once it has, her addiction is everything to her and you don't come even a poor second. If you threaten her addiction, Sally will attack you ferociously or drop you with a callousness which takes your breath away. Whatever she says when intoxicated, she is unable to love, as love is about giving. Sally can only take.

If you spend a lot of time with Sally you will be changed. Without realizing it, you will start facilitating her addiction and losing sight of your own needs, rights and wishes. Your life becomes a dance around Sally, the aim of which is to avoid conflict. Living with an addict is an awfully long life, bleak, dull, unrewarding and sometimes very dangerous. Sally will use you up, and then, when she has got what she can from you, she will spit you out.

All this changes if Sally goes into recovery. It isn't the original Sally who is abusing you, it's her addiction. There are proponents of various methods of achieving recovery from addiction, but in my career I found the best results were achieved by Alcoholics Anonymous, and by the similar 12-step organizations set up for people with addictions other than to alcohol. There are those who disagree, but I don't think that an addict can ever control her addiction. Abstinence is in my view the sine qua non. Achieving sobriety while working the steps of recovery is a powerful (and free) form of psychotherapy which enables a person to work on every aspect of herself and her way of living. Most of the rest of us never get to do this in the helter-skelter of everyday life, which means that an addict in solid recovery is often a very special and rewarding person to know. It's an interesting challenge to work out who the ten people are you have met in your life and most admire. I've taken that challenge and found that five of the ten are alcoholics or addicts in recovery. You don't have to be an addict to become a wonderful person, but it certainly helps, so long as you achieve sustained recovery. If you don't, you're toxic.

There's a lot more to say about addiction, but as there is a host of other books on the market dealing with the issue (including one by me entitled *Dying for a Drink*), I'll leave it at that for now.

You

If you're one of the world's givers (and if you are, this book is aimed at you), the chances are that your main threat is yourself. Your double standards are outrageous. You excuse everyone almost anything, while subjecting yourself to savage criticism the first time anything goes wrong or you fail to live up to your self-imposed standards of perfection. I would suggest that you ask yourself whether you would say to any other person what you routinely say to yourself. No? Well, my view is that cruelty and abuse aren't OK, even if they are only inflicted by you on yourself. Just a thought.

Are you worried that you may be toxic to those around you? I doubt it, as most toxic people never consider their effect on others, but there's no harm in checking. If you have friends or family who are kind, care about you and are confident enough to be honest, ask them what effect your behaviours have on them. Be ready to hear uncomfortable truths, and be slow to challenge or justify. Just listen and ask questions later. Remember that criticism of a behaviour isn't a rejection of your value as a person. A feeling isn't right or wrong, it's just a feeling, so if a friend says you make her feel bad she means just that; not that you are a bad person.

People who seem to be toxic, but aren't

In order for someone to harm you, that person needs to affect you, by making you feel uncomfortable and by changing the way you behave. Joe is a larger-than-life character, loud, bombastic, opinionated, but with a soft centre. He's a sheep in wolf's clothing. He can be clumsy sometimes, but he's surprisingly sensitive and as soon as he sees that he has upset you he backs off. He has a heart of gold and any upset you feel is short-lived. You don't find yourself running around after Joe because despite his bluster, he really doesn't demand anything of you. When people talk about Joe, they tend to sigh and look heavenward, but with a smile. He is fun to have around; just don't take him too seriously. Joe comes in many types and forms, the point being that he doesn't coerce you into anything and he doesn't purposely, repeatedly or consistently cause you unhappiness or stress.

Well, that's my list of toxic people. It isn't definitive; it simply reflects the types of people and behaviours who or which have made my patients ill over the years. I'm sure you have other examples of the types of people who have caused you the most problems. The point here is to be alert. Notice the people who harm you and make real decisions over what to do about them rather than being a cork tossed around on an ocean of toxicity. Part III of this book may help you with that. But first, here is a checklist of some of the danger signs which indicate that you may be in the presence of a potentially toxic person. Remember, this really only matters if you possess several of the vulnerability factors listed at the top of this chapter.

- You feel exhausted, unhappy or stressed much of the time when with them.
- You often feel obliged or pushed by them to do things you wouldn't do by choice.
- You've been hanging around for them for years without your relationship really moving forward.
- You often feel guilty about not doing more for them.
- You often feel judged or humiliated by them.
- You often do things to keep them happy in order to avoid trouble.
- They demand more than they give, and you give more to them than to anyone else without being able to say why.
- You feel you have to be especially careful not to upset them.
- You don't feel you have choices with them.
- You are fearful of them.
- When you're with them, you ignore your own needs.
- You spend a lot of time fearing what they will do next.
- You can't say what you really mean or feel when with them.
- You can't give an example of them doing something out of conscience (e.g. helping someone else).
- You feel trapped a lot of the time with them.
- Unflattering stories about you, which you can trace back to them more than once, get back to you.
- You frequently make special allowances for them.
- You often find yourself facilitating or colluding in behaviours you wouldn't tolerate from anyone else.

5

Toxic places

It doesn't take very long for a few toxic people to pollute an entire place or organization. During my career, I saw a steady stream of employee casualties from the same toxic companies. They just kept coming, from the 1980s when I started in psychiatry, right up to the mid-2010s when I retired. I have no doubt that the conveyor belt keeps rolling on to this day. This is despite the fact that the managers who were making their employees ill in the 1980s had mostly retired by the turn of the millennium. How come?

The answer is that an organization quickly takes on a culture which is formed by a few influential people and is kept going by the culture-bearers who come after them. While many of these influential people are at the top of the company or service, not all of them are. It is hard for a junior employee to repair an organization which has become toxic, much easier for a junior but persuasive individual to pollute a place which was previously healthy and productive. Once the culture has been formed, it tends to persist. Positivity, creativity and real accountability breed more of these qualities. The same is true of cynicism, negativity and disempowerment.

Much of what follows refers to places of work, but clubs, voluntary organizations, hostels, schools, colleges and even churches can equally be afflicted.

In Part I, I discussed some of the factors which influence the way people behave. All of these apply to how an organization functions, in particular (see Chapter 3) the role of leaders.

Leaders

While a good leader can have an enormously positive effect on the functioning of a team, the converse is also true. Toxic or incompetent leaders create toxic places in which to work. Unfortunately, there seem to be far more bad leaders than good ones, particularly in public services. The agenda in the NHS, the police, ambulance and fire services, schools and social services is set by politicians, who are mostly in my experience fairly cynical individuals and poor leaders. It is therefore no surprise that I saw so many patients from these services in my career, made ill by the toxic influence upon them of their political masters.

As you would expect, my patients were the best people, the good honest triers.

Leaders who create toxic work environments first forget the purpose of leadership, which is to facilitate productivity. It's human nature to want to change a workplace in your image when you take over. Or maybe it's canine nature. Move a dog to a new house and the first thing he'll do when let out into the garden is to urinate around the perimeter. He's marking out his territory and unfortunately most new leaders of organizations do the same when they take office, by changing almost everything. They probably tell themselves that they're helping, but they aren't. What they are really doing is inflating their egos by putting their mark on their new territory. They mostly don't consider that such change is toxic. Every employee of the NHS is familiar with the changes in structure that occur every time a new government takes charge. Every one was accompanied by a fanfare and promises that services would be improved. They weren't.

I'm not saying that change shouldn't happen; of course it must if an organization is going to adapt and survive in the competitive modern world. But change is like surgery: you should have it when you need it, but not when it isn't essential. People work best in a familiar environment, within structures they understand. Rapid change harms efficiency by disrupting the well-being of the workforce.

Bad leadership is characterized by unclear and conflicting directives and goals. Say it takes 30 minutes to make a widget well, 20 minutes to knock one together sloppily. You are told you must improve quality while producing three widgets an hour. Hmm, I don't think so. It's even worse if you are told to 'Do a better job with the widgets', without being told whether 'better' means higher quality or greater volume. Bad leaders treat requests for clarification as evidence of stupidity or impertinence, so the workforce just muddles along, hiding its mistakes when it can.

The opposite of this style of leadership is real accountability. In our sadomasochistic society, this word has come to mean 'when something goes wrong, find out who was responsible and punish him'. The result is fear, paralysis and deteriorating performance. The real meaning of accountability, a concept apocryphally created at Harvard Business School in the 1950s, is 'As leader I will delegate this area of responsibility to you. Because you don't have my knowledge or experience you will make mistakes. That's OK so long as you acknowledge them and learn from them.' The practice of real accountability improves efficiency and morale in equal measure. Toxic workplaces don't practise it.

Bad leaders issue vast quantities of top-down directives without explanation, usually accompanied by some kind of threat involving the dire consequences of failure to comply. Fear abounds and paranoia flourishes. Rumours that this is all leading to a round of compulsory redundancies start circulating. Most of the directives require a considerable outlay of time which isn't reflected in any reduction of other duties or any increased reward. The workforce isn't consulted and has no idea of the meaning or purpose of the directives. They feel beleaguered and powerless. The leadership is autocratic and remote and there is no chance of anyone being able to feed back problems or issues to them.

Just when the organization is beginning to recover from this upheaval, another reorganization is announced. All the changes so painfully absorbed are now swept aside, and objectives and targets are shifted.

There is a real belief among some leaders, particularly those in charge of public services, that this is the right way to operate. I know because I've listened to their rationalizations. The gist of it is that if you stir up the organization sufficiently, making it a really challenging environment, the weaker employees will leave and those who stay will be the strongest and most resilient. They're wrong. In fact, there is good evidence that the opposite happens. The best and most diligent workers take on each new half-baked directive as gospel and give it their all. Eventually they become disenchanted, exhausted or depressed and in due course they leave. What is left is the sludge, those who have cynically found a way around the system, who are able to look good and compliant while in fact doing very little. These cynical opportunists know how to meet their targets and so get promoted. Eventually they become the new leaders.

And so a toxic culture is formed. Its fuels are blame, fear and avoidance. Blame someone else, keep yourself secure by making others afraid of you and avoid real responsibility by playing the system.

It doesn't have to be like this, but it will be if the leader is all about him or herself, fails to nurture those under him or her, and subscribes to the belief that 'nothing must ever go wrong'.

Unofficial culture-setters

These tend to be charismatic and persuasive individuals. They make friends readily, have an easy way with humour and are good at getting others to buy into their world view. If you contradict or oppose them you will tend to find yourself excluded from the group. They are a crucial key to how an organization functions. The trouble is that it's much easier to be a critic than an architect, and so most of these influential people use their skills negatively in a way that works against the organization. It is worthwhile for leaders to identify culture-setting people within their organizations and attempt to bring them onside. This doesn't happen in toxic places and so, if you want to work honestly and positively, you'll find your efforts hampered by these people. They'll make fun of you for working too hard, or criticize you for making the others look bad by doing too much. You will increasingly feel you have only two choices: become cynical and negative like the culture-setter or become an outcast at work.

A particularly destructive type of culture-setter is the saboteur. This person is motivated to stop any endeavour from succeeding and a few of them can bring an organization to its knees. He is a master at manipulation and gameplaying and he always uses his skills destructively. He tends to be driven by anger and resentment, though this may not be apparent when you first meet him. He feels he should have achieved more and has been prevented from doing so by unfair forces within the organization, the world, or people generally. He predicts the failure of any endeavour and is delighted when he is able to point out that he was right. You can't work effectively with a saboteur, as he will ensure that anything you do which could be really helpful will come to nought.

It only takes a few destructive culture-setters to make a workplace toxic.

Lack of teamwork

As I explained in Chapter 2, a well-functioning team achieves more than is possible through its constituent individuals working alone. This doesn't happen in toxic places because their members have no common goals or interests. Each person feels that she's out for herself, competing against rather than cooperating with her peers. A 'dog eat dog' atmosphere prevails in which colleagues eye each other with well-deserved suspicion. Again, I have heard it argued that such internal competition improves productivity. It doesn't, for the reasons I outlined earlier, but bullies, who thrive in toxic environments and so collect in toxic organizations, enjoy watching you scrap it out with your peers. It's a kind of modern version of bear-baiting, I suppose, the so-called sport so popular with the ruling classes in the sixteenth to eighteenth centuries.

In poorly managed organizations, well-meaning structures intended to improve the performance of the team can make things worse. A good example is '360-degree appraisal'. The idea is that the functioning of all levels in the hierarchy can be improved if everyone rates each other. You are rated by your bosses, your peers and those who report to you. Sounds great, really egalitarian and informative. The problem is that it doesn't work. It just increases stress, reduces openness and honesty (are you going to give constructive negative feedback to somebody who is about to rate you?) and fosters pretence and avoidance.

The same is true for official structures and labels that supposedly encourage good teamwork, for example 'Investors in People'. It's really clear which organizations care for and nurture their employees or members, and they aren't the ones with fancy certificates on the wall. They are the ones with leaders who really take an interest in the welfare of their employees. You can't care for someone by filling out a bit of paper. Like the boundary invader who protests how little he is asking of you, distrust any employer who claims too loudly to be great to work for. This isn't being cynical, it's just reserving judgement until you have real evidence. A quiet private chat with a couple of people at the bottom of the hierarchy will tell you more than a hundred certificates.

Working in a really high-functioning team can be an immensely rewarding experience. Unfortunately, there aren't many of those about, though there are plenty who claim to be. Working in a toxic 'team' is awful and over time is likely to make you ill unless you become toxic yourself or develop effective strategies to protect yourself. More on this in Chapter 9.

Bureaucracy

One of the ways in which leaders seek to leave their imprint on an organization (or country) is by introducing more bureaucratic structures. The idea is that if you introduce more rules and measurements of compliance with those rules, you will be able to stop bad things happening in your organization and make it a better place. No you won't. You forget that time spent filling out forms is time taken away from real productivity. The world has known this for at least two millennia. The most famous ancient quote on the subject is often attributed to a Roman soldier called Caius Petronius, writing around AD 50:

> We trained hard, but it seemed that every time we were beginning to form up into teams, we would be reorganized. I was to learn later in life that we tend to meet any new situation by reorganizing; and a wonderful method it can be for creating the illusion of progress while producing confusion, inefficiency and demoralization.

Brilliantly put. Unfortunately, it seems the words are actually those of novelist Charlton Ogburn, penned in 1957. Well, darn, don't you hate it when facts get in the way of a good story? The truth is, though, that people have been moaning about unnecessary bureaucracy and change as far back as Roman times (see Pliny the Elder, a Roman governor, diarist and political commentator at around the time of Christ) and beyond. The best antidote I ever witnessed was early in my career at a psychiatric facility where the managers and consultants set up a 'forms committee'. Nobody could design a new form without persuading the committee that it was both necessary and as brief as possible. The trouble was you had to apply to the committee by filling out a form . . .

When organizations become really toxic, they often attempt to hide their uselessness behind a proliferation of bureaucratic structures. In my view, a useful question to ask of any organization you are considering joining is 'How many forms do you have which are not required by law?'

Sexism, racism and other prejudice

I touched on the topic of prejudice earlier in the book, but it needs a mention here, because some places are institutionally prejudiced. It's part of the culture and has been that way for ever. You can't argue with prejudice, it's just prejudice, and if you try to legislate against it you merely drive it underground. It tends to abound in toxic places, because somebody has to be blamed for failure and the poor-quality people running the show have to protect their egos by defining themselves as better than whichever group they are discriminating against. When an organization is falling apart, those within it tend to blame whoever they can define as 'other'. Working in such a place will undeniably be toxic, unless you enthusiastically embrace the endemic prejudice yourself.

Constantly increasing demands with decreasing resources

'Efficiency' is a popular buzz-word among many managers, and rightly so. In the increasingly fierce competition of the modern world, every business or service needs to ensure that it is as efficient as it reasonably can be. The issue needs to be revisited regularly as new ideas, technology and competition emerge.

The problem is that most organizations don't analyse themselves and the market, don't look carefully at what they can reasonably dispense with while avoiding undue harm. They don't analyse how much more can be squeezed out of existing resources without doing damage to those resources. They just keep on ratcheting up the demands while salami-slicing the resources year by year.

An example I heard some time ago was of a car production line. Demands to increase the number of cars made per week were gradually ramped up while human resources were equally gradually pared back. To begin with, productivity increased slightly – that is, more cars emerged from the facility. As demands rose and resources continued to fall a plateau was briefly attained (see Figure 7). But then, when resources were reduced just a tiny bit more, the collapse was sudden and catastrophic, with very few cars being made and the business collapsing.

I've seen this happen more times than I care to remember. The worst thing is that you lose your best employees first. They try to keep going, achieving the impossible without any source of support, until they break down and end up in my office, while the backsliders remain, pretending to keep the show on the road until inevitably the whole thing eventually collapses in a heap.

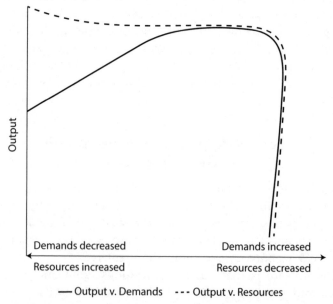

Figure 7 **The ratio of output to available demands and resources**

The opposite of this was a technology company that used to get me in to do some work on reducing the harmful effects of stress. Their managers could be found at 6.30 p.m. sending their most diligent workers home. They realized that it is good cold business sense to protect your best workers from burnout, to encourage them to pace themselves. I wish I could say that they maintain this policy to this day, but I can't. My services were dispensed with in a round of economic cuts, and I'm told that they now ratchet up demands and cut resources with the worst of them. They aren't doing very well . . .

There is one thing you can do to increase output without increasing resources, and that is to increase the autonomy and empowerment of your workforce. There is ample evidence that a worker who feels heard, empowered, with a real stake in the organization, is more productive than one who does not. There is of course a limit to how far this can be taken. At the end of the day somebody has to make the big decisions and not everyone can agree all the time. Nonetheless the model illustrated in Figure 8 works.

Empowerment, autonomy, a feeling of being invested in the organization and the availability of sufficient resources all increase productivity, while increasing stress (above a healthy level) reduces it. Not an easy balance, that, leading effectively while fostering these positives. And you thought management was easy!

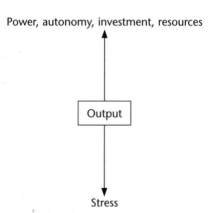

Figure 8 Factors affecting output

Shifting the finish line

Toxic organizations can't be trusted. Their employees or members know this and are understandably cynical about everything they hear from on high. They know that once they have met one target, that target will just be used as a starting point for the next one, as evidence that the initial target was too low. The finish line is never reached because, as soon as it's approached, it is shifted back. It's like that dream where you are being pursued down a corridor, but as you run down it, the passage extends further and further in front of you to infinity.

This model, which is integral to the culture in many organizations, is highly toxic. The only people who survive it unscathed are the cynics, the manipulators and those highly competitive types who run at an unsustainable level for a while, gambling that they will be promoted out of the toxic mess at the bottom of the pyramid before they go under.

The reward desert

Being rewarded nourishes a person, allows her to bloom. Toxic places offer no rewards, just threats, fear and punishment. Rewards don't only come in financial shape, though a pay increase is always welcome. Even more effective are praise, trust and involvement. Bad managers praise nobody and involve only members of their impenetrable clique. If you work in a stressful environment where you receive no praise, where you aren't involved and aren't trusted, you are in a toxic place. Beware, because unless you look after yourself very carefully, you will be at risk of succumbing to stress. (If it has already happened, have a look at my book on the subject, *Stress-related Illness*.)

Camouflaged toxicity

Some of the most toxic people whom I or my patients have ever encountered have worked for charities or been heavily involved in a church. Don't get me wrong. I'm not giving an anti-religious, secular message here. I'm a believer myself who was schooled for ten years in a Catholic monastery by some lovely Christian people. What I'm saying is that membership of an organization founded on good principles is no guarantee of goodness.

The way to evaluate any organization and the people within it is by what they do, not what they say or what their title is. Do they really practise Christian principles of kindness and selflessness? Are they dominated by cliques who leave you excluded and disempowered? Do you feel uncomfortable and unwelcome, an outsider, despite having been there for a year? Do you smell the whiff of prejudice and hypocrisy? Are the most influential people within the organization apparently motivated more by self-importance than by charity and the love of their fellow human beings?

Be careful, you may be in a toxic place in camouflage.

6

Toxic families

This chapter is short, but I could write a book on the subject. The family is the unit upon which society is built, a wonderful, nurturing group based on love, instruction and support, the direction of that support varying over time. But it is also the unit responsible for much of the unhappiness and damage inflicted on people. The thing is that, while you can ditch friends who aren't friendly, you're stuck with your family. A little toxicity goes a long way when you're exposed to it in your most formative years, or all the time. The same types of toxic people do damage to their families as they do to anyone else, but the effect of their toxicity is magnified by the binding effect the family provides. A toxic person is many times more toxic if he is your parent than if he is your acquaintance.

If you want to find out more about 'families and how to survive them', I suggest you read the excellent book of that title by Robin Skynner and John Cleese. For now, I'm going to emphasize a few of the ways in which some of my patients have been harmed by their families. You may find that what follows repeats a certain amount of material found in earlier chapters, but I think this is worthwhile, as families were at the heart of the problems suffered by so many of my patients.

Gameplaying families

Gameplaying as a family culture gets passed down the generations. If as a child you are taught that power and advantage are gained through the covert manipulation of situations and people, the chances are that you will practise these strategies as an adult. You may not even realize that you are doing it; it's just a way of life. But gameplaying as a family culture does real damage. There isn't any real spontaneity or intimacy in a gameplaying family, only jockeying for position. As a parent, if you coerce your children to do your will not by issuing direct instructions but by using guilt or guile, you may enjoy a quiet family life, but you are making it very unlikely that they will grow up able to enjoy happy and stable, spontaneous and intimate relationships in the future. Most likely they will find themselves using the same manipulative behaviours on others which you practised on them – or the opposite may be true; they may go through life always putting themselves last and being prey to the games of others, or worst of all, to depressive illness.

Enmeshed families

Enmeshed families are those in which the relationship between two family members becomes so close and over-involved that other family members are excluded, and the enmeshed parties lose their individuality. Gerald's mother Nancy dotes on him exclusively. He is her pride and joy and can do no wrong; the golden boy. As a result Nancy's husband Peter is effectively excluded, and after many unsuccessful attempts to rekindle the closeness he and Nancy enjoyed early in their marriage, increasingly he spends his time drinking in the potting shed. Gerald's sister April is essentially left parentless, realizing all too well that she isn't the favoured one: she's the spare part, needed by nobody. The toxic results of this dynamic on April are obvious; having never been valued as a child, she is unlikely to value herself as an adult, and thus becomes a ready victim of the users and abusers of the world.

The results for Gerald may be less obvious, but are nonetheless definitely negative. The stifling and exclusive bond with his mother will prevent him from learning the give and take necessary for future relationships to succeed. The 'helicopter parenting' exhibited by Nancy removes the chance for Gerald to learn from experience or to develop his own real preferences and skills. Nancy sorts out everything for him, causing Gerald to grow up lacking resources, initiative and patience.

It's a difficult balance, this: how to be a loving, responsible and active parent without becoming enmeshed with your children. It's really important though; children from enmeshed families don't do well. Nobody said parenting was supposed to be easy.

Scapegoating families

Let's take the family I described above, under 'Enmeshed families'. There's a kind of unhappy stability in this set-up. Every family member has learnt to accept the status quo, having realized that trying to change things is pointless. But what if April comes home with a boyfriend? He takes one look at the dysfunction which is April's family and asks her what the hell is going on here. Now, a really honest answer will involve every family member accepting their responsibility for contributing to the mess the family is in. Easier just to blame Peter. After all, he simply drinks all day. If it weren't for him being alcoholic, we would all be fine, one happy family. You may think it strange that when Peter tries to cut down on the booze, drinks are left out for him and the family discourage his efforts at recovery. But it isn't so strange; he's occupying the valued role of scapegoat and the family don't want to lose that function, lest they have to confront their own problems.

Scapegoating can be very resistant to change. Some of my patients who seemed to me to be kind, genuine and lovely people had spent their lives assuming that every misfortune was their fault. Very difficult to shift that belief.

Bullying families

I've already talked about the harmful effects of bullying, but those effects are particularly toxic within the family, because the victim is essentially captive. The effects are worst when a parent (or, God forbid, both parents) bullies their child. The irony, as I've said before, is that the bullied child, lacking any real self-esteem, grows up totally devoted to the bullying parent. To the day he dies, the bully is able to rely upon the ceaseless devotion of his adult offspring and to coerce them to do his bidding.

Sorry, but if in contrast you're a good, giving and loving parent, that probably won't happen. Your kids will be off into the world as soon as possible, experiencing it to the full with the benefit of the confidence and positivity your good parenting gave them. By the time they reach adulthood, the last thing your kids will want is to hang around for long periods with their boring old parents. Life never was fair, was it? And it isn't only the bullying parent to whom the grown-up child acts as an unpaid servant. She will tend to pick up a whole retinue of people who take advantage of her good will.

Before I stir up a storm of outrage, I accept that some offspring of good, loving parents do spend time with their parents; a really happy extended family is a wonderful thing. It's just that it often doesn't work out that way.

Of course, it isn't only parents who bully their kids. As the years go by and parents become more vulnerable, their sons and daughters sometimes bully them too. Such elderly people seem to me to have forgotten, in their devotion to their offspring, that they themselves matter too. Just because you're old shouldn't mean that you have no rights, or that your preferences shouldn't be taken into account.

It's worth mentioning in this context the effect of rage. The rages of the person with explosive personality issues aren't really bullying, as they aren't a deliberate attempt to inflict suffering or subjugation on the victim. On the contrary, the enraged person typically feels powerless, oppressed and out of control. Nonetheless, the effects can be the same; family members will collude by protecting the explosive person from anything which might enrage him. The dynamics of the family shift and the narrative becomes 'Don't do anything to upset your father' (or whoever the explosive person happens to be). Such families live in fear, and the adult offspring of explosive parents tend to run their lives principally on the basis of fear: 'If I ever take a risk, I'll be punished. Best play safe.'

The worst form of bullying is abuse, sexual abuse being the most toxic. I touched on the issue earlier, and I won't deal with it any further here. If you or somebody you care about has been physically or sexually abused as a child and is suffering the effects to this day, I strongly advise you to consider looking for appropriate psychotherapy. Speaking to your GP is a start. There is also a wealth of good literature on the subject. Just type 'Adult survivors of childhood abuse' into your search engine or look for the topic at your local bookstore or library.

Right-fighting families

I borrowed this term from the popular American TV psychologist, Dr Phil McGraw. It refers to relationships in which there is no respectful sharing or exchange of views or preferences, just a set of contests to prove that you are right and your opponent wrong. The thing is that the topic under discussion usually involves feelings. Feelings are neither right nor wrong, they're just feelings. So, to say 'two plus two equals four' is fair enough (probably; there are mathematicians who may argue the point). It's a fact. To say 'what you said to me was upsetting and offensive' leaves you open to counter-argument; you are claiming a fact when you are really talking about a feeling. What you and I define as offensive may not be the same. However, to say 'I was upset about what you said to me' should brook no argument. My feelings belong to me and I am their only arbiter. Right-fighting families ignore this distinction and any difference becomes a metaphorical fight to the death.

The exchange may go like this:

'You upset me.'

'No I didn't, I was just telling the truth.'

'Yes you did, you were mean.'

'No I wasn't, you're just silly and oversensitive.'

'You're an opinionated idiot.'

'Look who's talking. What about when you . . .'

And so it goes on. There is no attempt to gain information from each other, just the single priority to win the argument and be justified. I have witnessed families who do little else but right-fight. Those family members who are less verbal or assertive withdraw and nobody learns anything from anyone. Children brought up in such an environment are able to fight their corner, but not to empathize, compromise or negotiate effectively in relationships.

Families without nurturing

Above all, a child needs a secure attachment with at least one constant, reliable, nurturing person, and preferably with several. If this doesn't happen, because of the illness or death of one or both parents, or because the parents are unable or unwilling to nurture their kids, the effect on the child is toxic. As he grows up, he will be unable to relate warmly to others, and any relationship he engages in is likely to be self-centred or insecure. A parent who does not persuade her children they are loved is setting a time bomb which will explode later in their lives. Fortunately, many kids are immensely resourceful. I've known plenty who have apparently emerged unscathed from childhoods spent with cold, affectionless parents through the healing effects of a kind and loving teacher, aunt, uncle, grandparent or family friend.

Families affected by addiction

I've mentioned addiction in the context of toxic places, but it can't be left out of a chapter on toxic families either. Addiction doesn't only affect the addict. The toxic effect of the disease has an impact on the whole family. This includes anyone living in the same household, but the effect is not surprisingly greatest on the children of alcoholic parents. If you or someone you care about falls into this category, I recommend that you read the book *Adult*

Children of Alcoholics by Janet Woititz. I think you will recognize the picture of a person who takes too much responsibility, tries to keep everyone happy all the time and tries to put everything right. Addicts, until they go into recovery, do immense harm to those around them. A family with an active addict in it is toxic. If you are in such a family and you think you're unaffected, you may be wrong. If you doubt what I'm saying, talk to someone outside the family who isn't afraid to tell you the truth.

You may feel that some of this chapter is rather repetitive of what has appeared earlier in this book. Apologies if you do, but the point here is that the same people and situations who make people ill in other areas of life also do so in families. More so, in fact, because families are such a powerful source of influence, both for good and for bad.

7

Toxic situations

Some situations in life are designed in such a way that, if you hang around for long enough, you're going to get hurt. This is true regardless of whether the people involved are toxic or not. It's always worth looking out for whether any toxic people are involved, though, because if they are, their toxicity is probably at the root of the problem and you'll need to act accordingly (see Chapters 4 and 11). I won't rehash the problems such people cause here, but it is worth us also spending a bit of time on situations that tend to cause people emotional harm. Some people seem to get into such situations all the time, whether through naivety, uncritical kindness or lack of foresight. Giving the situations you meet in life some thought before rushing headlong into them is an important part of staying happy and healthy.

I will keep this chapter brief, but if you want more, have a look at my earlier book, *Stress-related Illness*. The subtitle, 'Advice for people who give too much', may hold a clue.

Conflicts, moral dilemmas and double-binds

On the whole, a single stress doesn't make a person ill, but if there are two stresses working in opposite or conflicting directions, illness is often the result. If Tom is single and wants to be employee of the year, he can work all hours and achieve his goal, no problem. Then he gets married and his wife has a baby. Tom wants to be the perfect husband and father, involved in night-time feeds, home early enough to be involved in bathing the baby and a source of real emotional support for his wife Emma too. But Tom and Emma now have a mortgage and three mouths to feed, and so it is crucial that Tom should maintain his upward trajectory at work.

Can't be done. Not possible. Sorry. Something has to give. If no compromises are made, what will give is Tom's health.

Particularly difficult are conflicts involving moral priorities. You are at a dinner party at which your host expresses a view you believe to be racist and repugnant. You know that she is a person who is sensitive and easily hurt. Do you contradict her view and state honestly your strong opposition to her position, or do you sit on your hands and through your silence imply agreement with her bigotry? Knowingly to cause hurt or to retreat from everything you believe in? I now live in the Deep South of the USA and occasionally meet this dilemma (along with a lot of kindness and generosity), though to be honest I also witnessed racism back home. I'll let you know later on how I manage it.

Double-binds are conflicts people create, usually but not always for manipulative purposes. Your mother asks to be allowed to spend more time looking after your baby, but she gets tired easily and when she does, her migraine tends to flare up. She never sees this coming and you feel the need to avoid requesting too much of her. So you feel guilty either for denying her the joy of spending time with her grandchild or for setting off her headaches. Very stressful for you, as there is no obvious solution. Maybe there isn't supposed to be one?

Overwhelming demands and fixing the unfixable

Some 40 years ago a famous study looked at what made women susceptible to depressive illness. It was a remarkable piece of work in which every woman living in Camberwell who agreed to take part was interviewed. The researchers found that the single most toxic situation a woman could face was not death, disaster or divorce, but having three or more children at home under the age of five without family support. It doesn't matter if you are an unmarried mother trying to be the perfect parent in a tower block in Camberwell, or the CEO of a publicly listed company attempting to keep the share price up in a falling market. If you try to achieve the unachievable, it'll make you ill.

When the going gets tough, the tough get ill.

Life is full of unfixable problems. The most unfixable of all are people who don't see the need to change. Trust me on this; I spent the early part of my career trying to do just that. Later I came to realize that my role was to offer my patients insight and choice, not to impose changes, however beneficial they were likely to be. You can help a person to change direction if he is willing to, but if he isn't, the only result of your efforts will be frustration, resentment and eventually illness. I've met many people who have selected partners with obvious long-standing problems, only to be disappointed when those problems don't respond to efforts to heal them, but instead get worse over time. This isn't to say that a person can't change, he certainly can if he really wants to. But does he want to?

Peer pressure and taking sides

Group dynamics are complicated and often difficult to handle. While you may be able to stand up to the unreasonable demands of an individual, it is much harder to resist a group, particularly if you rely on the friendship of its members. If there is peer pressure to do something that you don't want to do, stress results. If this happens frequently or constantly, then the situation that is created is toxic.

A common form of this is pressure to take sides. Two friends are in dispute and each turns to you to arbitrate. You try not to take sides, but each of them accuses you of letting her down, of not being a real friend. So you lose one friend or both – and, as often as not, the rest of the friendship group too, as you become the bad guy for not being loyal. Very upsetting, very unfair. Very common.

Anger, hatred and prejudice

If you are an angry bigot, you'll thrive in situations and groups dominated by blame, prejudice and hate. If you aren't, such situations are extremely toxic. As I've said before, you can't argue with prejudice as it has no basis in logic. You can't compete with a spittle-projecting merchant of hatred; the power of the emotion is sufficient to demolish an office block. If you get in the way, you'll get hurt. If you live in a situation where these conditions prevail, you're in a very toxic place.

Loss and grief

Grief is toxic. When a much-loved and loving spouse dies, the risk of death of the surviving partner in the next year rockets. Grief may be a natural and necessary process to allow eventual re-emergence into the world, but don't let anyone tell you it's ever OK. It isn't. What does occur over time (I can't say how long, it varies so much) if you allow yourself to grieve is that you become free. Free to feel your grief when and in the way you choose to, rather than being constantly disabled by it. Free to feel the whole range of emotions when you choose to: including sadness, but also in other situations amusement, affection, excitement and yes, even joy. If you've suffered a recent loss, you may not believe this, but there is an end to it – not of the sadness, but of the total, constant blackness; that is temporary.

Major losses of all sorts are toxic in the same way grief over the loss of a person is. This includes the loss of a job, status, grown-up children or friends who have moved away, of home, money, health or marriage; whatever you hold most dear. In fact, it seems to me that divorce is at least as toxic as the loss of your spouse through death, as there is no culture or ritual to support you in your loss, just unpleasant solicitors' letters telling you what a monster you are. I know that solicitors have a job to do, but is it really necessary to increase people's suffering at this most vulnerable point in their lives?

Personal vulnerabilities

There is no point in me trying to describe all the situations which will be toxic for you, because it depends on your particular vulnerabilities, which are unique to you. They are partly determined by your genetics, but more so by your previous experiences. Adversity doesn't make you stronger; it makes you more vulnerable to situations later in life which, really or symbolically, are similar to those you suffered before. The earlier in your life you suffer a trauma, the more vulnerable you are to similar situations later on. So the loss of a parent when you are 12 makes you more vulnerable to depression in response to losing your job at the age of 40 than someone who has never lost a parent. While the death of a parent is very different from redundancy, there is a symbolic link; both represent loss of certainty, belonging and value. This is the phenomenon of resonance which I outlined in Chapter 1.

So there are a lot of toxic obstacles in life. Let's now look at how you can cope with them while remaining happy and healthy.

Part 3
COPING WITH TOXICITY

8

Principles for coping with toxicity – general

In November 2015, I retired from clinical practice and my wife and I emigrated to America. It is the land of her birth and a nation I have always admired, so I left with a song in my heart. Then, a year later, my adopted country elected a president whose behaviour and policies we both found repugnant. I felt alienated, duped and somehow betrayed by my neighbours, particularly because in the area of the Deep South where we live, most of the population is four-square behind their leader. How to cope with this situation, which I was finding toxic?

I decided that I would become involved in helping opposition movements, as that prevented me from feeling so powerless. I took to wearing a safety pin on my shirt, the symbol created in the UK to signify opposition to bigotry and intolerance in all its forms. At the golf club I had joined and into which I spent a year trying to integrate myself, I was asked what the safety pin was for. My explanation was greeted with stony disapproval, and then Jim spoke up for the group: 'Tim, you need to remember that you are a guest in this country and you should accept your hosts' decisions.'

So, what to do? Stay silent and through my silence imply assent, or continue to offend and alienate my peers? Here was a situation I could have found toxic. Those affable people who had welcomed me with such friendliness were at risk of becoming toxic to me, as I was being urged to acquiesce in views and attitudes which run against everything I believe.

My solution was to be strategic. I replied to Jim, 'One of the things I admire most about this country is its welcoming of free speech and acceptance of diverse views. I respect yours, but mine are different.' I kept wearing the safety pin, but I avoided arguments about whose political stance was right. When engaged, I moderated my tone as much as I could while being honest about what I believe. I accepted that I wasn't going to turn a bunch of elderly white male South Carolinians into a group of progressives, but I determined quietly to maintain my own identity. When I challenge, I do so gently, seeking small shifts rather than any about-face, and if I find anything with which I can honestly agree, I do so. I use humour and self-deprecation. If I'm asked a direct question I answer it briefly, respectfully and honestly, but I don't attempt to force my attitudes on those who don't welcome them. I've found a few people who share some of my beliefs. And I studied American college football, which is all the rage here, so that I became able to engage the interest of my peers.

It seems to be working. I'm viewed as that quirky liberal Brit, but as I challenge no one who doesn't welcome it, I'm no threat and so I'm accepted. Disingenuous? Cowardly? I say strategic.

This is an example of the idea I want to sell to you. Understand what you can and cannot achieve, which means understanding the situation you are in and the person or people you face. Take your time; be an observer until you really understand what is going on. Then, when you do, be strategic, not angry, and don't be a victim.

Assertiveness

Assertiveness is the opposite of aggression. My guess is that you know someone who is truly assertive. She doesn't shout or stamp her feet, she just quietly and firmly says what she has to say. She argues only when she has to. If challenged, she focuses on the substance of the challenge, rather than engaging in any mutual mud-slinging. In the face of noisy abuse, she restates her case, refusing to be deflected by the chaff of conflictual argument. But she won't withdraw if she believes the issue is important, realizing as she does that conflict can't always be avoided. If there is anger in the air it isn't hers, but she won't be deflected or intimidated by it either. She never shouts, and if shouted at she waits until the shouting stops and then answers the substance of the challenge. Not easy to do when there's enraged spittle flying into your eye.

She tends to get her way in the end. Indeed, after a few early skirmishes, people very rarely try to push around an assertive person, as they come to realize that there isn't any point. Assertiveness is highly effective, one of the most important skills you can learn. So how do you learn it?

The answer is by observation and practice. Watch people who are really good at it and try to emulate them. Not the aggressive bombasts, but the quietly firm types. But here's the thing: if you have never been assertive, you're not going to be any good at it when you first start trying. So the most important ability that you will need to aquire while learning how to become assertive is to be able to fail well. Give it a go, mess it up, forgive yourself for messing it up and be kind and respectful of yourself when you're learning from your mistakes.

You'll feel like a fraud to begin with, that's inevitable. You're pretending to be assertive when you don't feel assertive at all. That doesn't matter, because of the principle: you become the way that you act. That is, if you act assertively, or try to, for long enough, you become assertive. Really, genuinely assertive. So keep going, keep learning from your mistakes, keep being kind to yourself.

Try to avoid becoming angry or aggressive, even if you feel that way; speak quietly and take your time. If you become enraged, ho-hum, there's another learning experience for you. Don't judge the outcome, particularly at first. The object of trying to be assertive is to practise this skill, not to achieve any positive outcome, at least to begin with. Results will come later.

And don't look for a round of applause from the object of your assertiveness. It takes a very strong person to acknowledge his errors and the person you are experiencing as toxic is very unlikely to be one of them. Much more likely, he will be angry or will ridicule you. It doesn't matter; you're not responsible for his reaction. What does matter is that for the first time, you are practising assertiveness. Don't accept his judgements of you; he's not objective, as he's railing against being stood up to for the first time, because he's not used to it. It's what you are trying to do that matters, not the outcome. Keep going and you'll get there in the end. You might start by trying out your more assertive approach on a trusted friend, telling her what you're doing and asking for her forbearance while you practise.

Setting boundaries

One crucial aspect of assertiveness is the setting of boundaries. This means being clear on what your limits are and sticking to them. The person pushing you to do what you don't want to do doesn't have to be happy with your refusal, she just has to accept it. Keep the same predictable limits all the time and eventually they will stop being challenged. When users or abusers are accustomed to getting their way, they won't be happy when you first change the rules, but stick to your guns and eventually they will stop testing your boundaries. So don't fall into the trap of looking for acceptance or approval of your limits. You won't get it, not to begin with.

If a person repeatedly makes you uncomfortable with her demands, you need to review your boundaries. What do you choose? Are you happy to compromise? If you're inclined to do what is asked of you, why? Are you really making choices here, or are you allowing yourself to be bullied into doing something you wouldn't otherwise choose? Is it time for you to stand your ground? Yes? Then start now; it'll only get harder if you put it off.

When the boundary invader is getting angry with you for starting to set boundaries, it's helpful to have something to say which is neutral, non-inflammatory. Don't express outrage at her unreasonable demands, but don't apologize for your limits either. Something like 'I'm sorry you're feeling angry with me' can work well. It's very different from 'I'm sorry I made you angry' or 'I'm sorry to let you down'. You didn't make him angry, she chose to be angry. You didn't let her down, you simply set a boundary; how she responds to it is up to her. This may seem like a matter of semantics, but it's important. You can acknowledge a person's feelings (and it often helps to defuse a situation to do so) without taking responsibility for that person.

In setting your boundaries, your prime responsibility is to yourself. If you don't respect your limits and needs, others won't either, and in the end that will make you of less use to those who really need you, as well as to yourself. But do give yourself sufficient time. This stuff isn't easy, particularly when a toxic person is challenging you.

Minimizing conflict

As I've already said, you can't, or shouldn't, always avoid conflict, but you can minimize it. The key here is to remain alert when involved in interactions. When all is harmony it's fine and dandy, but when there is tension in the air, make sure that you are thinking. Sometimes disagreements are affable, an interesting and mutually rewarding exchange of views. But at other times your differences are an obvious source of difficult emotion between you and those you are conversing with. Then is the time to ask yourself the following:

- Why am I engaging in this argument?
- What do I seek to achieve from it?
- How am I going to go about it?
- What are the chances of me achieving my goal(s)?
- What are the risks?

Let's take an example. You are in a coffee break in the office and two of your most bombastic and bigoted peers are discussing the need to stop all immigration, specifically that of people of colour. You find their racist rhetoric offensive. Do you accuse them publicly of being racist bigots? Do you stay silent? Let's ask ourselves the five questions above, and see what the answers might be.

- Why am I engaging in this argument? *Because they are being offensively racist and not to do so would imply my agreement.* OK, you need to say something.
- What do I seek to achieve from it? *To persuade them that they should be less racist, or at least to keep their more offensive views to themselves.* Really, you think they are going to drop a lifetime of racism just because you say so? If there are others in the room who share your views, you could seek to humiliate them by having several of you berate them together, but it's a risky enterprise, much more likely to lead to a schism in the office than to useful changes of attitude. But if you say, 'Hey guys, could you give it a rest, this stuff makes me uncomfortable,' you might just be able to shut them up. Chances are they'll challenge you with something like 'So you want the country to be full of black people then?' You don't have to engage in the argument. You can

sidestep with: 'I don't want to discuss it, guys, just take it up after work will you? Thanks.'

- How am I going to go about it? *I'm going to make it clear that I don't share their views and try to stop them from airing them when I'm around.* Well, you've done that already. You may have to set the boundary I suggested above several times if it keeps happening, but the chances are they'll get the message in the end. You're not going to sit and listen to their racist claptrap, much less be drawn into it.
- What are the chances of me achieving my goals? *Pretty high, if I limit myself to getting them to understand that I don't agree and stopping them from going on like this in front of me. If I set myself the task of changing their minds, my chances would be slightly less good than of being elected pope.* Correct.
- What are the risks? *There's a high risk of stoking up damaging office conflict if I engage in full-on argument. That would harm the team. As it is, there is a risk they'll pick on me for refusing to share their views, but I can live with that, because there are enough like-minded people in the office I can turn to if I need support. In any case, the only alternative is to say nothing, and I'm not going to do that, as it'll only go on. I'm not going to listen to this stuff every time I have a break.* Good for you. You've thought strategically and done what you need to do in order to set assertive boundaries, without stoking up unnecessary conflict.

Thinking strategically takes some practice and you won't always get it right. Remember to be generous and respectful to yourself when you get it wrong, while being honest that you did so and learning from your mistakes. Try not to retreat into exclusive blame, such as: 'They're idiots, it was them that caused the argument, not me.' Try to think logically and analytically after the event when things go badly.

Avoid right-fighting. This means recognizing the point at which a discussion changes from being a useful exchange of views into a conflict in which neither party is really listening to the other, but both are instead restating their own position with increasing anger and volume under the misapprehension that the other party will eventually see sense. No they won't, because they aren't listening, and neither are you. Try to remain cool enough to recognize this point and then to withdraw. Something like: 'Oh well, I suppose we'll have to agree to differ' or 'I'm getting a bit het up with this discussion. Could we stop and revisit it tomorrow please?' can work well. You can't argue with someone who refuses to argue.

If you're good at humour, use that in order to get your views across without stirring up conflict. If you're not, don't try it in the heat of battle. If you decide to try to change someone's mind, do so gently. If you can achieve just a slight shift, it will be real. If you try to force someone into a complete turnaround it won't. The result will either be conflict or acquiescence. Either way, you will have achieved no real changing of minds.

Dealing with feelings

Feelings are just feelings and they belong to the person feeling them, not to anyone else. They are neither right nor wrong, they are just feelings. So listen to them and try to respect them, whether they are your feelings or someone else's. Don't try to change them or argue with them. This can be difficult if they are directed at you.

Lenny's girlfriend Wendy says she's upset that he can't take her out to dinner on Valentine's Day because there's a work function he has to attend. Lenny could cut Wendy off before she's finished what she has to say. Isn't she being unreasonable? After all, it's his career we're talking about. He doesn't have a choice about the work event and it's not fair to be criticized when it's not his fault. But Wendy hasn't been criticizing him, at least not at first. She's just saying what she feels, which is that she's upset at not getting the evening she was hoping for. These are her feelings, not Lenny's, and they belong to her. It would be better for Lenny to listen to them. If he waits for Wendy to express fully what she feels, making supportive and regretful noises along the way, Wendy will probably conclude herself that, regrettable though it is, the work commitment has to come first.

If Wendy works herself up into a lather and accuses Lenny of not caring about their relationship, what then? The answer is to separate the feelings from the facts. Something like this will do: 'Wendy darling, I'm so sorry this has happened. I understand you being upset. I'm upset about it too. I was really looking forward to it and I do care about us, a lot. But there really isn't anything I can do about it. It's not fair that they've done this to us.' Lenny has validated Wendy's feelings while reiterating his lack of choice.

'That's rubbish, if you really cared you'd tell your stupid boss that you have a prior engagement,' replies Wendy.

Don't argue, but don't agree to what isn't true either: 'I'm sorry you feel that way, but I really do care.' Here Lenny is on firm ground because he's talking about his feelings, which belong to him. Wendy can choose not to believe him if she wishes, but she can't tell him he's wrong. He is the arbiter of what he feels.

Your own feelings need to be treated with equal respect, especially by you. If you find that you are insulting yourself for having them, challenge the bully who has taken up residence in your head (and who bullies only you). 'Oh, I'm just being silly, stupid, oversensitive, ungrateful, pathetic, selfish, etc, etc.' Really? Would you speak to your dearest friend like that? No? Then don't speak to yourself like that either. Try to look at your worries and feelings as if you were a wise and sympathetic friend. Are your feelings telling you something valid? Do they mean something, or do you just need to reassure yourself? If that's the case, do so with respect and sympathy.

So dispute facts if you wish, but not feelings. Listen to them, share them, welcome them. If you feel overwhelmed by the incessant torrent of feelings which issue from a person, that's another issue, one I'll deal with later.

Sharing

Many toxic people try to isolate you (see 'gaslighting' in Chapter 2). That's a major source of their power. The antidote is obvious. Don't allow yourself to be isolated. It isn't a betrayal to share feelings, dilemmas or upsets with friends and family, though the toxic person will tell you that it is. The vast majority of wives talk to their girlfriends about their husbands, often in quite intimate detail, and I can't see any real harm in this so long as it doesn't lead to anyone being ostracized, humiliated or bullied. Men, at least in the UK, seem in contrast to keep things more to themselves, mostly preferring to discuss less personal topics such as sport, politics, jobs and money with their chums. There may be a bit of sexual stereotyping here, but I've seen this caricature of the sexes confirmed over and over again in my consulting room.

So don't be upset that your wife talks about you to her friends; it helps to prevent you from driving her insane. Don't be upset that your husband never discusses you with his friends; it doesn't mean he doesn't care, he's just being a bloke. Men, if you're really up against it, you need stop being a bloke and seek someone supportive to talk to.

If you're at your wits' end and don't know what to do, talk. If you're dealing with someone toxic, consider the power of the group. I'm not talking about spreading malicious gossip, but of simply refusing to let yourself become isolated, a victim; instead, share your experiences and feelings with others on the basis that the wisdom of a group is greater than that of any individual in dealing with challenging situations (see the 'Desert Survival Test' on page 17).

Two caveats here. First, tribalism and narrator bias. When you tell a friend about an emotive situation you are doing so from your perspective. The object of your narrative doesn't have the opportunity to give his side of the story. So, because the information going in isn't objective, the answer that comes out may not be either. In any case, your confidante will naturally be inclined to see things from your point of view, being on your side, in your 'tribe'. As she doesn't have to deal with the person you're talking about, her view is likely to be a more extreme version of yours, unless she is remarkably perspicacious in her judgements. 'What a bastard, you need to divorce him' may make you feel better, but it isn't necessarily the best advice.

Second, the power of the group may protect you from toxic people and situations, but it can have a malign effect too. If the dominant person in the group, the de facto leader, has an uncharitable or angry agenda, you may find yourself pushed by the group to act in a way you would otherwise reject as too unkind (see the sadistic guards in Chapter 2, in the section on 'People in groups'). In the end, you have to make up your own mind and act accordingly. Believe me, those who exhort you to extreme actions will run a mile if things go wrong.

Helping

Helping others is one of the most rewarding and liberating actions you can take, particularly in the areas you find most challenging. 'We teach best what most we need to learn' is very true in my experience. If you keep your eyes and ears open, you can learn an enormous amount about how to deal with difficult people and situations while you are standing side by side with someone in the thick of it.

But don't be compulsive in your helping and don't always look for the obvious fix. Stand beside the person needing your help, rather than offering glib advice that is neither needed nor asked for. Unequivocally warm support, caring, empathy and being available as a sounding board are as valuable to a person suffering from toxicity as formulaic advice is useless. When to help and when to hang back until asked can be a difficult judgement. No harm to offer support, but if it is declined then withdraw, while making it clear that you're there if needed. And don't try to solve a problem for someone unless he agrees that it is a problem and have asked for or accepted your help to solve it. Compulsive helpers can cause chaos in a person's life by imposing solutions on situations for which they are poorly designed. If you're going to help someone, he is the boss, not you; listen to what he needs, not what you think he should need.

If you are asked for advice, don't be upset if your friend doesn't take it. Often it's necessary to hear somebody articulate an option before one realizes that one needs to do the opposite. Your advice shouldn't be an instruction, it should be an item on the menu from which your friend can choose. And if I learn, after the event, that when your friend hasn't followed your advice, which in retrospect has proven to be right, you've said: 'Well, you can't say I didn't warn you. You've only got yourself to blame,' I shall arrange for you to be severely punished. We don't have retrospect in advance, more's the pity, so avoid being wise after the event.

Responsibility

Toxic people often try to make you responsible for them – for how they feel (see 'Dealing with feelings' on page 93) and for how they behave. So an important principle for surviving them is deciding for yourself the bounds of your responsibility.

It may be fairly obvious, but you are responsible for what you do and say. If you do things which are antisocial or say things which are mean, whether drunk or sober, you should expect criticism and possibly sanctions. But what may be less obvious is what you aren't responsible for. You are responsible for the words you say and the intention behind them, but you aren't responsible for how a person responds to them.

Alison tells her boyfriend Rory, who is pouring out his fourth gin and tonic from her drinks cabinet, that she is uncomfortable with how much he's drinking. Rory flies into a rage, throws his glass at Alison and breaks a mirror. The next day he explains that he took Alison's words as a humiliating criticism of him as a person. He accuses her of belittling him and labelling him as an alcoholic.

It is crucial that Alison should have none of this, however much she wants to soothe Rory's feelings. What Alison said the previous evening was accurate and factual. The fact that Rory interpreted her words in a way which was far from her intention was his responsibility, not hers. He must pay for the mirror, because he threw the glass which broke it. 'But you made me throw it, by winding me up,' argues Rory. Mm-mm, no way. Think again, chum. Your reaction to a person's words is your issue, not hers. You threw the glass, you pay for the mirror. And if you pull a stunt like that again, we're finished. At this point it's appropriate for Alison to do her impression of a brick wall. No negotiation, no discussion: agree or walk. This is a tough thing to do for someone who isn't naturally assertive, but if she lets this issue slip, believe me things will get worse over time.

Be very clear about the boundaries of your responsibility, particularly if you are often in the presence of a person who tests them. Check your sense of these boundaries with someone you trust, who isn't involved and who is confident enough to challenge you if necessary. However caring and generous you are, don't take responsibility for any other adult of sound mind. You may help and support, but don't be responsible for other people. Be very wary of anyone who tries to make you feel responsible for them, their actions or their feelings.

9

Principles for coping with toxicity – some specifics

In the last chapter we looked at some general principles which apply to all relationships, but which are particularly important when dealing with those who pose a risk to our health and welfare. In this chapter I want to build on those principles, adding some specific actions and techniques you need to consider if you meet these people and situations quite often.

Serenity

You need plenty of this if you spend much time in the presence of a toxic person or in a toxic place. The key to achieving it is summed up nicely by the 'Serenity Prayer' of the excellent 12-step movement (originally penned by the theologian Reinhold Niebuhr), which goes like this:

> God, grant me the serenity to accept the things I cannot change,
> The courage to change the things I can
> And the wisdom to know the difference.

Whether you're religious or not, I think you'll agree that this is spot on. It's really back to the issue of strategy. There's no point in shouting at the storm like King Lear. Life isn't fair and people certainly aren't. Every happy person in existence looks for opportunity, not fairness, and the converse is also true: if you are determined to get what you deserve, you're going to be a bitter and unhappy person. In any case, be careful what you wish for; what you deserve, given the fact that you aren't perfect, may not be the same as what you want. The truth is that life presents you with a pile of poo from time to time, but at other times it will award you a bouquet you haven't earned. Deal with the smelly stuff as well as you can and enjoy the flowers. Nothing in life lasts, and 'this too shall pass', whether it be good or bad.

Above all, don't waste your time trying to punish the architect of your misfortune. Punishment doesn't work (see Chapter 1) except for those who don't deserve it. The toxic person you're trying to get back at will never 'learn her lesson', she'll just take your efforts as a challenge. And the chances are that she'll be better at punishment than you are, having spent most of her life perfecting her skills of manipulation and intimidation.

So how about the last line of the serenity prayer? How do you gain this wisdom, other than through the gift of God? The answer, I think, is by taking your time, thinking, sharing and being a good observer. Remember, you'll be much more persuasive if you take a gentle approach, nudging rather than shoving, suggesting rather than demanding, respecting rather than criticizing. In the end you may need to draw yourself to your full height and stand your ground (see 'Responsibility' in Chapter 8), but fight only when you have to.

In most situations it's about being a good negotiator. This means respecting the other person's point of view, but articulating your own as well and finding a position which, though not ideal, is acceptable to you both. This really is important, and it's worth practising your negotiation skills. As before, this means letting yourself get it wrong and then learning from your mistakes. Watch couples who are good at negotiation and learn from them. They are respectful, they listen, suggest, shift as appropriate, persist and compromise. Couples who are good at it can negotiate a compromise, such as what they are going to do today, without ever finishing a sentence, communicating through the movement of eyebrows, shoulders or hands, mmms and aahs, reaching a mutually satisfactory position in 20 seconds flat. It's beautiful to watch. Learn from them.

If the toxic person won't negotiate, then you must consider what sanctions you have at your disposal. This isn't punishment, it's refusing to be a victim. If your partner does nothing for you, why are you cooking for him and doing his washing? You don't have to be angry, just firm, such as: 'I've been thinking, I seem to be doing everything around the house. I don't want to become resentful and you don't deserve that as I haven't said anything up till now. So how about you doing your own washing and us alternating who cooks supper?'

Yes, I know he'll be horrified, but so what? At least it's opened up a discussion about roles. You haven't criticized him so there is nothing for him to defend, just the motivation to start negotiating. You hold all the aces in this hand. Not easy, but the longer you leave it the harder it will be. There are opportunities for change in your relationship, but not if you avoid stirring things up at all costs. If you decide against this, you must accept the status quo, as it's the one you chose.

Understanding and accepting yourself

With apologies to those of you who have no interest in sport, I'm going to use a golfing metaphor here, as I think it's apposite. Until you learn how to get out of bunkers, you'll keep landing in them. Once you get the knack, you'll end up not having to use it very often.

It's the same with people and situations. You'll keep meeting them until you learn how to deal with them. The reason is simple: toxic people prey on vulnerability. So if you're going to start dealing with such people more effectively, you need first to identify your particular vulnerabilities. They may include low self-esteem, lack of confidence, shyness, naivety, an uncritically generous and forgiving nature, the tendency to put others before yourself, an empathic aversion to the suffering of others or any of the other traits listed in Chapter 2. You may find it difficult to construct and guard appropriate boundaries, and you may lack a sense of entitlement.

When engaging in introspection it's important that you are honest with yourself. What are you really like, not how would you like to be? If you have a kind and sympathetic family member or friend who is also honest and perceptive, ask her what she feels your vulnerabilities are. Why do you feel the way you do in the presence of the person or situation you find toxic? Are you experiencing resonance with earlier experiences, or are you identifying too strongly either with the toxic person or those she is affecting?

Keep it simple. Like most things in life, your nature and vulner-abilities are probably neither unique nor very complicated. Once you have some insight into what you are like, try to change a little. Use the principle of 'you become the way that you act' (see Chapter 8). Behave a little differently, moving in the opposite direction to your nature. Go against the grain a bit. So if you lack a sense of entitlement, try to behave in a slightly more demanding fashion. Again, don't expect approval from the object of your changed behaviour, you won't get it. And don't expect to do it well; you're just practising. If your attempt to set boundaries fails, it isn't a failure, it's a success, because you've started to try to change. Results will come later if you keep at it.

You'll notice that I've used the words 'a bit', 'a little' and 'slightly' quite often. This is being realistic. You'll take some time to make the substantial changes you need.

And here's the most important principle of the lot: accept who you are. Sure you have weaknesses and vulnerabilities – we all do – and by all means work on changing what you want to. But don't discount yourself as boring, worthless or undeserving. You aren't. You're just you. Some people will like you and others won't, but that doesn't diminish your worth or your entitlement. You need to treat yourself with respect. If you don't, you'll wear a metaphorical label on your head declaring to toxic people: 'Use and abuse me, I'm worthless'. It's difficult if you've never asserted yourself, but start trying now.

Understanding the toxic person

I'm going to look at how to deal with the different types of toxic people in Chapter 11, but for now, suffice it to say you need to understand what you're dealing with. It's not enough just to survive, you need to understand this individual. Why is he behaving this way? What are his motivations? Do you know anything about his background, or can you find out without being too intrusive? Understanding where he is coming from may give you a clue as to how to deal with him. For example, say he tends to behave aggres-sively towards you, more than he does to anyone else. You know that he was bullied at school. Do you remind him of the person who bullied him? Is he intimidated by you? Would emphasizing your gentleness and lack of threat be helpful? If on the other hand he's aggressive because he was brought up to believe that aggression is the best way to get what he wants, maybe standing up to him and setting firm boundaries are the priorities.

The point is, it's valuable to try to understand what lies behind the toxicity of the people who do you harm in order to develop an effective strategy for coping with them. As always, talk about it to someone you can trust if you can.

Timing

Toxic people tend to make you angry, frightened or upset, or all three. When you're feeling this way is not the time when you are best advised to react to them, as you are likely to be responding to your emotion, not to the needs of the situation. And whatever you do, don't react when you're under the influence of alcohol. That can be difficult, as speaking your mind can seem like a great idea when you have had a few. But don't. Ever. While your confidence increases with consumption of alcohol, your judgement and skill decrease. You need your wits about you when managing someone who is toxic.

Whenever possible, and appropriate, if you're struggling with strong feelings, wait until tomorrow to tackle the issue with which the toxic person has confronted you. If she is demanding something, put her off with a response like 'I don't know, I'm a bit too tired to think about it right now, let's discuss it tomorrow.' This is difficult too, because by then the wind will no longer be in your sails, you'll feel inclined just to forget about it so as to avoid conflict. And anyway it's difficult to find a way of bringing it up, because the time and context have passed. But if you have been badly affected by someone, particularly if it isn't for the first time, you'll need to deal with it at some point. You may use a phrase like: 'Hey Bill, I've been thinking about what you said last night. It upset me, which I don't think you meant to do, but I don't want to do what you were demanding and I find it difficult to refuse you.' You haven't accused Bill of anything or given him much to take offence at, but you have made your feelings and boundaries clear.

In contrast, if you are feeling fairly calm and in control, be alert for opportunity. The time when everything is up in the air can be an opportunity to change things. The word 'crisis' derives from ancient Greek, and means literally 'a time of opportunity and decision'. When the crisis arrives, as it tends to from time to time around toxic people, be awake to the opportunity if you can. Say Martin has upset a number of his friends with an offensive remark. They are remonstrating with him and he turns to you, saying, 'They're being unfair. You're my friend, stand up for me.' You could do so, as it will calm the situation, but you'd be missing an opportunity. Instead you could say, 'Martin, I know you didn't mean anything by it, but what you said sounded pretty bad. You do sometimes wind people up, you know.' Then, when someone else chimes in with a further criticism of Martin, you can ask them to back off. Thus you've made a point to Martin while also demonstrating loyalty to him.

In these situations, try to remain alert and act strategically. If you are wound up, angry or upset yourself, leave it until tomorrow.

Commentating

One of the most powerful ways of changing behaviour is to describe it. Group psychotherapists use this strategy a lot. If I'm running a group in which things are getting rather heated, I may interrupt to say: 'Hey everyone, just stop for a second. I want to make sure I've got this right. Ed just said he was feeling angry that Thomas didn't turn up last week. Thomas didn't say why he didn't come along, but suggested that Ed was an idiot for complaining. Is that right?' This will usually result in Thomas backing off a bit, because when put as plainly as this, his behaviour seems unreasonable. If Ed just blusters about how insulting Thomas is being, a predictable exchange of insults will follow which gets no one anywhere. By describing the interaction, I'm giving both Thomas and Ed a chance to look at it objectively, rather than jumping into the fray.

If the group is particularly rowdy, I might shout above the hubbub: 'Stop. What is going on here?' Ed will pipe up, 'Thomas was just being an idiot,' and Thomas will respond, 'No I wasn't, Ed's the idiot!'

'No, that's not what I meant,' I say, 'I mean what is going on, really? I'm asking you to stand outside the group and look at what is actually happening here.'

This tends to stop the torrent of insults and gets people thinking and looking at themselves and each other. As likely as not Julie will say, 'I think Ed was upset because he broke up with his girlfriend last week and I don't think Thomas likes to be criticized.'

And so the group goes on, in a much more productive direction than if it degenerated into mutual mud-slinging. I've given an example here of how a therapist may intervene to change the dynamics of a psychotherapy group, but you can use the same strategy when you're dealing with someone difficult. Reacting to a person who is speaking aggressively to you, you could respond aggressively and profanely, but it's likely to be more productive if you stop the situation in its tracks with a commentary, such as: 'Simon, it seems you're angry with me. What's it about?' Once you have real information from Simon, rather than just a stream of emotion, you're much more likely to be able to deal effectively with him. In any case, once Simon realizes he's coming across angrily, he may well settle down and behave more reasonably.

When a situation becomes so heated that you don't know what to do, try to halt its progress. Stepping outside the situation and commentating on your understanding of it can be a potent way of achieving this. I could write a whole book on this topic, but for now the message to take away is: if you can see that an interaction is moving towards the cliff edge, stop going in the direction you've taken. Look to understand where you are before you try to make any further progress.

Looking for beauty

Conflict and toxicity are ugly. If you focus only on this aspect of life your whole world will seem like a dark place. So focus on something or someone else if you can. There is beauty around you, so find it. I shall be looking specifically at awareness in the section on mindfulness in Chapter 10. For now, the message is: look beyond your immediate surroundings and find what is good out there.

By beauty, I'm not really talking about physical beauty, though that is undeniably agreeable. I mean people, places and situations that make your shoulders relax, remove your frown and make you go 'Ahhh . . .' Have a think about this, and when you're feeling afflicted make some active choices to move towards what and who you experience as beautiful. If you're stuck sharing an office with Neil, a toxic person, this may seem impossible, but it isn't. You can do what you need to do with him but give him nothing about yourself. Then when Sylvia the delightful tea lady comes round, engage her in conversation for a while. Her sunny and generous disposition is the antidote to your colleague's toxicity. Five minutes with Sylvia will protect you from five hours with Neil. At the end of the day, reflect on Sylvia, not Neil.

When you think about who you are and who you want to be, identify (see Chapter 1) with Sylvia. She may not have the most important job at your workplace, but she is your real world, if you attend to her and those like her, rather than the Neils of the world. If God comes down here again, he'll be serving the tea, not chairing the board meeting.

Taking charge

Many toxic people, particularly bombasts, are impossible to take charge of. They'll just shout over you if you try. So don't try, it's pointless. It's not the bombast you need to take charge of; it's you, your choices and your situation. So if Sarah is firing off in all directions, you may try to calm her down, to placate her or to please her, but you'd be missing the point. Sarah is doing what she does; the situation is irrelevant, you don't have to fix it. Better to move away, leave her to rant at someone else and go and attend to something more productive. A parting comment like 'Sorry you feel like that, Sarah, but I've got to go, I'm running late' may suffice. You've taken charge of your situation and minimized the toxicity. You haven't engaged in a battle with someone who specializes in battles and you haven't allowed yourself to be a victim.

Where is your locus of control (see Chapter 1)? Are you dependent on the words and actions of others to determine how you feel and what you do? If so, you need to start thinking strategically about what you can change. You are responsible for your welfare, not for ensuring that other people are always happy with you or approve of you. Say you are an alcoholic in early recovery. Don't accept an invitation to a dinner party with a group of heavy drinkers. Sure, they may be disappointed in you, but not for long; they'll get over it and will soon come to accept what you will and won't do. If they don't, they aren't real friends. Focus for now on friends who are also in recovery (for example, in AA) and broaden your horizons later, when you feel stronger. There, you've achieved an internal locus of control; you've altered your environment to fit your needs, rather than having your actions determined by others.

Honesty and objectivity

Try to minimize your value judgements and avoid misattribution (see Chapter 1). The fact that Veronica is impossible isn't the point. In what behaviours is she impossible, and what strategy are you going to use to deal with her? Whether she is a good or a bad person really isn't your business; your actions in response to her challenges are. If you spend a lot of time fuming over Veronica's unreasonableness, it's your fuming which is the problem. The world is full of Veronicas, and many more who sometimes act like her. Deal with them.

When interactions with someone always seem to go the same way, leaving you feeling bad, look closely at your role in them. Remember, it is human nature to tend to put a positive glow on our actions and a negative one on those of others. So, with sympathy and respect for yourself, try to look honestly at your part in what goes wrong. If you have friends who can be honest and not take a polarized view, ask them to help you look at what you could do differently to avoid always being left feeling the way you do after talking with Veronica.

Using cognitive dissonance

Again, this is about being strategic. Just because Paula wants something to be true doesn't mean that it is true. If she is always demanding that you do things for her, it may be that she believes you depend on her friendship and have nothing better to do. So be unavailable, organize other things when she expects you to be around, get in touch with other friends and have them call you when you are with her. This is much more effective than being overwhelmed by her demands, or becoming angry or defensive. You are recognizing the belief that drives her challenging behaviour and introducing contrary evidence, thus hopefully shaking her certainty that your sole purpose is to be at her beck and call.

While increasing the cognitive dissonance of the person you experience as toxic, you need also to reduce your own. The reason why you tend to let Paula overwhelm you with her demands is that you don't believe you are worthy or entitled just to be you. You have to be always proving your usefulness. So consider stopping this, and instead seeking out those friends who you know accept you as you are. Speak to yourself as you would your dearest friend. Would you expect her always to be rushing around doing the bidding of the nearest boundary invader? If not, then don't expect it of yourself either. You are reducing your cognitive dissonance, by giving yourself evidence that you are entitled to more than you had assumed. As always, sharing your thoughts with friends you trust can be very helpful.

Looking for meaning

If Victor Frankl could find meaning in being incarcerated in a Nazi death camp (see page 14), you can find meaning in your situation too. Look at the wider context of your life. If you are trapped in a toxic workplace, look at why you're doing it. If your job pays you more than the minimum wage, you're doing it either to furnish a better future, or to provide more for yourself and/or your family right now. It isn't the toxic job which is the meaning of your life, it's all the other stuff. Do what you have to at work, but don't define yourself or your life by it; focus on the rest.

Or maybe you love your career, but don't enjoy social events. That's OK, you're an introvert whose contribution to the world is mainly occupational. You don't have to be all things to all people. Find the meaning in your life, not in the life of the person someone else says you should be.

Avoiding prejudice

As I've already made clear, prejudice, by definition, is not open to reasoned argument. If you enjoy prejudice, who am I to argue? Go and fill your boots. Many people enjoy nothing better than having others agree with their half-baked pontifications. The fact that other people are agreeing with you doesn't make it true, though.

But if you face prejudice which you don't enjoy, which threatens you or your essential beliefs, get as far away from it as possible. Find another subject which is less incendiary, or seek out other people who take a broader view. Or, if you're stuck with it, don't engage. Switch off, give non-committal responses.

Reducing learned helplessness

It may be worth at this stage going back and re-reading the section on learned helplessness in Chapter 2. If you feel that you have no control over your life, the world or other people, it's a feeling you have learned, probably from quite early in your life. In order to change, you'll need to learn the opposite. This means first recognizing that it isn't your fault. You're this way for a very good reason. But you can change, by engaging in a set of cognitive experiments, that is by testing out against reality your theory that you have no influence on the world.

'Nobody will be interested in what I want' is your hypothesis. For example, what to have for dinner. Are you sure? Have you asked? Try it. 'How about fish tonight?' Say nobody responds to your request. Don't leave it there. Ask why not. Is someone allergic to fish? Or is it just that they didn't hear you because they aren't used to you giving your opinion? As likely as not, your follow-up enquiry as to why your request had been ignored will lead to your choice prevailing. So in this case, your hypothesis is disproved. People are interested in what you want. Reflect on that. Keep doing it. Don't accept the assumption that your choice will never matter. Keep challenging the assumption until it changes.

This is the basis of cognitive behavioural therapy (CBT), the most frequently employed and arguably the most effective form of psychotherapy used today. Find your unhelpful beliefs and assumptions and challenge them. If trying to challenge your own learned helplessness with the help of friends doesn't work, you may need to go to your GP to seek a referral for CBT.

Challenging perfectionism

Remember the Isle of Wight study of attachment and abandonment in Chapter 2? At least for parents, good enough is better than perfect. And the same can be true in many other areas of life, though I would probably tweak the statement slightly to say very good is better than perfect. It's fine to strive to be as good as you can be in whatever you're doing, just don't expect to reach perfection; it is neither real nor sustainable. The person who runs the first mile of a marathon in a perfect four minutes won't win the race.

This principle is especially important when dealing with toxic people, because they tend to pick on your imperfections in order to gain power and influence over you or to bully you. The point to remember is that a criticism of something you've done or failed to do, however valid it may be, isn't an attack on your whole worth. You can acknowledge a weakness or failing and continue to be a worthwhile person.

If the person you face is attacking you as a whole person, by saying for example 'You're just useless,' he is a bully or a sadist, unless there is some valid mitigation for what he said. Get away if you can. Attacks like that on the integrity or worth of a whole person, rather than a particular behaviour, are an assault. In my view you should think long and hard before forgiving and forgetting such an attack, as you would if someone punched you on the nose. And then, only if and when the perpetrator has acknowledged and taken responsibility for her misdeed.

Dealing with family

If your family don't show you love, turn to those who do. Remember my suggestion that a mother is someone who is motherly, and so on. If the person who really mothers you – that is the one who gives you unconditional love and support – is your best friend, turn to her in times of need. If your parent merely takes from you, makes demands and manipulates you, rather than giving you anything, consider erecting more effective boundaries with him or her. If you are a Christian, you can obey the commandment to honour your father and your mother without allowing yourself to be bullied or abused by them. Honour, in this context, I take to be the giving of respect as a human being worth neither more nor less than yourself. It's OK to hold a sense of duty towards your parents, but only if it doesn't make you ill. Put yourself in the equation when you are deciding what to do. Stand outside the situation and try to take an objective view of the balance of needs. If Helen, in the introduction to this book, did this she would clearly see that, on balance, she should not drive her mother to her appointment, but should tell her to get a taxi. Not ideal for her mother, but on balance right.

What about toxic marriages? Here I come up against a brick wall and I really can't give you definitive advice. Being a Christian myself, I'm not going to advise anyone to leave their spouse, as that would be sacrilegious of me. But have a look at the Christian marriage vows (or those of your faith or philosophy). Those I took promised 'to love and to cherish'. Of course, we all have our off days, but if there hasn't been any loving or cherishing in your marriage for a long time, that isn't marriage as I understand it.

I'm not telling you to leave, but if your spouse gives you only misery and illness, then make a fuss, create a crisis, insist on change, demand if necessary that the two of you seek outside help (maybe through the organization Relate, or with a marital therapist through a referral from your GP). That seems to me to be the only sensible way for you to give your marriage a chance. If you are religious, and are in turmoil because you want to leave your spouse but feel it's wrong to do so, go and talk to your priest or religious leader. If you pray, pray now. If you're not religious, talk to wise and moderate friends – not those who tend to extreme or facile solutions, but those who listen and are good at weighing things up in a mature fashion. Don't let yourself be isolated under the premise that what goes on between spouses should remain private. There's nothing disloyal about seeking support and unbiased wisdom.

Developing leadership and dealing with poor leaders

By leadership I don't simply mean being a leader at work or in sport. I'm referring to skills in motivating and persuading people to your way of thinking. I outlined these in Chapter 3 and I won't repeat them here. But when dealing with toxic people and situations it helps if you are persuasive, both in trying to change the behaviour of the person or people who are causing the problem and also in recruiting others in the group to the effort.

Don't try to win quick battles. Better to nudge people slowly towards change. Make suggestions softly but repeatedly and consistently. Unless you have a receptive audience, keep it simple and your aims realistic. If the situation isn't very challenging, or if in contrast you face a real crisis, you can be a bit more ambitious and try being fairly directive, but if what you face is a mixture of opportunities and threats, be circumspect and rely on soft skills of persuasion.

For example, if you own a shop which is doing well, employing happy and motivated staff, you can be fairly directive in managing them. Likewise, if a fire breaks out, there's no time to seek a consensus view; it's a crisis and you need to call the shots. But if the shop isn't doing so well and some of the staff are better than others (which is the situation for most shopkeepers), you will need to take a softer, more consultative approach to leadership. The same is true when dealing with groups of people in the rest of life. Unless the group you lead is very easy and receptive, trying to persuade gently and slowly works better in most non-crisis situations.

By the way, being gentle doesn't mean being taken advantage of; make sure your expectations are clearly stated and your employees know you want those expectations met. That's not being hard, it's being helpful. The number one reason people fail is because they're not given the information they need to allow them to succeed.

Bad leaders are very destructive, because of their power. If you have the choice, that is if it isn't going to cause real hardship for you or your family, consider moving on if you have a toxic boss. I know that I have advised you in general to try to avoid making value judgements, but with leaders I think it's often worth making an exception. I've treated enough diligent and non-judgemental people who have been made ill by a bad boss to know that you need to make some judgements about leadership, and to act accordingly. If you can survive comfortably with a bad boss, using some of the strategies I've already mentioned, all well and good, but if you're being seriously affected by your boss, look at your options rather than just suffering in silence. There are some very toxic people who find their way into positions of power, probably more of them and more toxic the higher up the echelons of power you go.

Having said that, there are some terrific leaders around: kind, nurturing, creative and insightful. If you find one, stick around her for as long as you can. In my view a good boss is worth more than a few pounds in your salary.

You may be able to 'manage up'. The boss you find toxic may be overwhelmed and flailing around because he's drowning in his own inability to cope with the demands he's faced with, or because he's being pressured by his own bad boss above him. If you can see a clearly better way of operating, you might raise it, diplomatically, as a tentative suggestion rather than a directive. You may find that offering to take on a task leads to a reduction in work and hassle in the long run, because there is less mess to clear up afterwards, in which case both you and your boss will be happy.

Look for opportunity when dealing with your boss, not for fairness or how it should be. Be strategic (yes, I know I'm repeating myself, but it really is the key). What I'm suggesting here may not be easy and may not happen overnight, but it's worth it in the long run. Stick with it. Take it slow. Keep track of what you try, what works and what doesn't. Measure your progress and celebrate your successes.

Dealing with toxic places

Places where toxic attitudes, practices and people predominate usually suffer from poor leadership, and so the principles I've just outlined are equally important here. If the culture of an organization is institutionally toxic, I'm sorry, you're cooked. There's nothing I can suggest other than to leave. But is the whole place really that bad? Are there some good people who have become silent through learned helplessness? Maybe, by seeking support from each other, you can insulate yourself from the madness, reminding each other that you are OK. It's remarkable how a group of supportive people can survive the most horrendous circumstances through the power of group support and affirmation. This is why many demanding workplaces set up support groups for their workers (I've attended a number of these in mental health institutions and each was very helpful). So whether your workplace is toxic or just very demanding, seek out the support of like-minded peers. Look particularly for people who make you feel better. Really reach out, don't just wait for others to help you.

Detoxifying and detoxifiers

Which brings me to people who make things better. These are the individuals who heal others who have suffered the effects of toxic people and places. Find them, and when you do, hold on to them if you can. Who are they? They are people with love.

I don't mean romantic love in this context, but love of one's fellow human beings. As I outlined in Chapter 3, such people listen; they are genuine, warm (without being possessive) and empathic. These people genuinely love and care about others and their positive influence is immense. While the best psychotherapists have these qualities, you can find such people anywhere. Hang around them if you can, and if appropriate, turn to them when the going gets tough. Choose your friends carefully and try to befriend people who have at least some of these qualities at least some of the time. Nobody is perfect and we all have our off moments, but in looking for people to hang out with, look mainly for kindness.

Look for situations and places which heal you and try to include them in your life. If a massage is what makes you feel better, get one from time to time, even if you can barely afford it and with three small kids there really isn't time. It's in everyone's interest that you stay emotionally in one piece, and if that is what it takes to survive the toxicity in your life, do it.

Are you a healer? You'll know, because if you are, you'll tend to attract a lot of vulnerable people and people with problems, particularly those with fragile, narcissistic egos (see Chapter 4 – these are the people who feel so badly about themselves that they depend on the approbation of others to feel OK, thus coming across as conceited and self-centred). If this is your situation, good for you; there's a special place in heaven waiting for you. But in order not to go under with the weight of the emotional demands put upon you, you must have effective boundaries. You need to say 'no' from time to time. You can't heal everyone and every misfortune. Pace yourself, and treat yourself as the valuable resource you are. Don't promise what you can't consistently deliver; for example, don't tell anyone that you'll sort out their problems. Their problems are their own, not yours. By all means be of assistance and offer support, but don't try to make everything right. Promise less than you can comfortably deliver and leave some space in your life just for you.

Dealing with toxic situations

I clearly can't deal with every type of toxic situation you'll ever face here, but in addition to what I've outlined in the last two chapters, here are a few pointers.

Focus on what is possible, what you may be able to achieve, not on perfection. Remember that good enough may be better than perfect because it's real and sustainable. Make active choices, rather than letting yourself be abused as a passive victim. Where there are conflicting priorities, look for balance. Choose a course which, while it may not be ideal, is good enough to allow you to cope with both.

Refuse to take sides unless you want to and choose to do so. In fact, make a point of it. While it's annoying when someone refuses to side with you, one tends to accept it if they're consistent. As soon as someone starts to denigrate a mutual friend or acquaintance, saying 'I hear what you're saying, but I never take sides on principle' will tend to stop them in their tracks, particularly if you reassure them that you'd do the same if the other party said anything about them. Be known as the neutral, the Switzerland of friends.

Escape from anger and hatred if you can. If such feelings are yours, accept them, but try not to act on them. Feelings are just feelings, neither right nor wrong. Don't engage with prejudice – don't argue with it or buy into it.

If you're bereaved, grieve. Don't try to chase it away, avoid it, distract yourself, accelerate it or keep it to a timetable. Feel it, stay with it, seek support, share and talk about it if you can. Cry when you feel like it, but don't judge yourself if you don't. If you don't actively try to stave it off, the grieving process will happen as is right for you. Then wait. In due course (I can't tell you when) you'll achieve the freedom to feel sadness when you choose to, rather than finding that it brings you to your knees at random, inopportune moments. Eventually, life will again take on a texture where sadness is mixed in with happiness and the whole gamut of other feelings which make up life.

10

Coping with toxicity –
three important skills

Coping with toxicity is difficult and requires a lot of energy, determination and persistence. To survive, you'll need to become good at staying calm and present, avoiding engaging in unnecessary battles and combating gameplaying. In this chapter I'll show you how to achieve these goals using the principles of relaxation, mindfulness and transactional analysis.

Relaxation

Relaxation exercises can be immensely powerful if you persevere with them, allowing you to reduce your arousal to a level which allows you to function calmly in toxic environments. The following exercise has already appeared in my earlier books, so you may be familiar with it already. There are many variations on the theme, and the thing is to find the one that works best for you. There are several relaxation exercises commercially available as audio files, or on CD or other spoken word media. Some people benefit from yoga techniques they learn in a group setting. Others find that following a written set of instructions helps them better, by allowing them to do the exercise at their own pace with their own mental imagery. What follows is just one example of such a technique, but one which many of my patients have found helpful, particularly those struggling to cope with difficult relationships.

Whichever way you choose to do the exercise, the essential point is that it needs a lot of practice. Though a few people pick it up very quickly, for the majority relaxation exercises are a total waste of time to begin with. They don't work straight away, leading many to become disillusioned and give up on them. Some people even feel worse at the beginning, because doing anything and feeling like you're failing at it tends to make you feel tense.

But please do persevere, because when you master the technique you will find that it changes your life. You're doing it not to benefit from it right now, but as an investment in your future. The people who benefit most from relaxation exercises are those who put them top of their list of priorities and practise for at least half an hour every day, come hell or high water. If you hear that a meteor is going to vaporize your town in 24 hours, by all means take flight for the hills, but not until you've done your relaxation practice.

Looking back, I did relaxation exercises every day for about three years, not because I was unusually anxious but because I thought then, as now, that everybody could benefit from them. It took me about a month of daily practice for the exercise to be of any use at all. It was at least three months before I reached the stage of being able to use it when I was under strain, such as before an exam, because the most difficult time to perform a relaxation exercise is when you most need it, at times of high stress. In about two to three years I reached the stage where I no longer needed the exercise because I could switch on a relaxed state like a light when necessary. I'm a bit slow, as I'm told that the average time it takes to become that good is about nine months, but never mind, I got there in the end and it changed my life. I can tell you first hand that it's worth all the time and effort.

A relaxation exercise

Spend 20–30 minutes on this exercise.

1 Find a suitable place to relax. A bed or easy chair is ideal, but anywhere will do, preferably somewhere quiet and private. Once you are good enough at the exercise to find it useful, do it when you go to bed.
2 Try to clear your mind of thoughts as far as you can.
3 Take three very slow, very deep breaths (allow 10–15 seconds to breathe in and out once).
4 Imagine a neutral image. An example may be the number 1. Don't choose any object or image with emotional significance, such as a ring or a person. Let the image fill your mind. See it in your mind's eye, give it a colour, try to see it in 3D; if it's a

word, repeat it to yourself under your breath, many times over. Continue until it fills your mind.

5 Slowly change to imagine yourself in a quiet, peaceful and pleasant situation. This might be a favourite place, or a happy scene from your past. Be there and notice all the feelings in each sense: see it, feel it, hear it, smell it and taste it. Spend some time there.

6 Slowly change focus to become aware of your body. Notice any tension in your body. Take each group of muscles in turn and tense them, then relax them two or three times each. Include your fingers, hands, arms, shoulders, neck, face, chest, tummy, buttocks, thighs, legs, feet and toes. Be aware of the feeling of relaxation in contrast to how the tense muscles felt. When the process is complete, spend some time in this relaxed state. If you aren't relaxed, don't worry; you're just practising for now.

7 If you're doing the exercise during the day, slowly get up and go about your business. If it's bed time, just lie in bed until you drop off to sleep (this is when you're good at it; remember that to begin with it may not work).

At step 5, I want to emphasize that this isn't simply visualization. It is a multi-sensory experience. Let me demonstrate. You are imagining yourself on a beautiful Caribbean beach. Lovely. But that

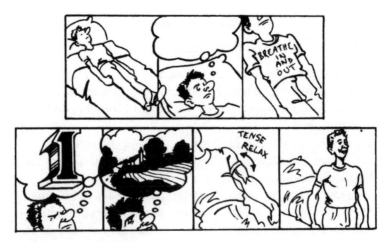

Figure 9 A relaxation exercise

isn't enough. Which direction is the wind coming from? Is it constant or gusty? What does it feel like when the sun goes behind a cloud? Does it get cooler? What does hot sun on sand smell of, and what is the smell of your suntan lotion? Is the sand soft or hard? How do the waves sound? What does your drink taste of? How far back does the grass start? Are the palm trees small stumpy palms or tall coconut palms? If they are coconut palms, are the coconuts brown or green?

You need to be there in every sense. This takes quite a lot of practice.

Don't hurry this procedure, and remember to practise. It will work, and when it does you'll be in a much stronger position to deal with the challenges you face.

Mindfulness

Again, readers of my earlier books will recognize this as a recurring topic. That is because it is a key to achieving real stability in life, whatever or whoever you face. Mindfulness, or mindfulness-based cognitive behavioural therapy (MBCBT), is a very powerful technique. Many would say that it's more than that – it's a whole way of life. It's a way of being which has been lifted from Buddhist philosophy and taken on by the cognitive therapy movement. I'm only going to touch on it here; if the concept interests you, I would suggest that you invest in one of the excellent texts on the subject written by an expert. I would recommend *Wherever You Go, There You Are: Mindfulness Meditation for Everyday Life* by Jon Kabat-Zinn, or *Mindfulness: A Practical Guide to Finding Peace in a Frantic World* by Mark Williams and Danny Penman.

In essence, mindfulness is beautifully simple, though in practice it can be difficult to carry out. Again, it's all about practice. There are only two main principles. The first is to stay present. Don't spend time ruminating about the past, except when you are trying to learn positive lessons from it. There is a time for reflection and learning from experience, but not repetitively, not resentfully and above all, not focusing on the injustice of it all. Once a period of reflection has led to appropriate conclusions, you need to come straight back into the present. Don't then revisit the past event unless something new has happened or changed, requiring further re-evaluation.

Equally, don't ruminate about the future unless you are doing real planning. When the plan is made, come straight back into the present. The stuff you're worrying about won't happen anyway, though something else will and there will be time to deal with that, whatever it is, when it happens. Your miserable meandering through your past and your future is a set of myths created by your distorted take on things. The only reality available to you is now, so experience it. This means being really conscious of your situation and environment, of everything you perceive and feel. What colour are the flowers you have just passed, what does the birdsong sound like, what colour are the bricks of the house in front of you? The list of sensations available to you is long, if you are really conscious and notice them.

The second principle of mindfulness is to stop fighting. That is, accept what is and can't be changed. In order to experience life we have to stop fighting it. So stop fighting the past, the future, unfairness, people, institutions, symptoms and most of all, your inability to administer just deserts to those who oppress you or those you love.

The mindful solution to toxic people is to experience them. Much of the stress and harm that comes from being in the presence of a toxic person or situation results from our railing against them. Boiling up with impotent rage isn't good for you, so work on bringing down your emotional temperature. Several eastern martial arts utilize the concept of defeating your opponent by appearing to submit to him. If you are unfortunate enough to be confronted by a man running towards you with a knife, the best thing you can do is to position yourself in front of a wall. As your assailant comes almost within touching distance, you step deftly to one side, allowing him to crash headlong into the wall. Through your quiet refusal to engage in combat, your opponent has defeated himself.

Prevailing, or at least surviving intact being stuck with someone toxic, will come not through struggle, but through the lack of it. This doesn't mean being a doormat and letting yourself be abused; it means achieving stillness in the face of toxicity, rather than flailing around uselessly. If you need to stand your ground, do so firmly but quietly. Stolid refusal to budge is much more effective than the shouting matches at which most toxic people excel.

I know this sounds easier said than done, and maybe it is, but mindfully accepting and experiencing people, however difficult they may be, is much better for your well-being than fighting them and, paradoxically, is much more likely to lead to you achieving an improvement in your situation. The quiet introduction of a thought has much more chance of changing a person's mind than full-on intellectual combat. If you become good at this you can often leave the other person believing that he has come up with the thought you introduced. Mindfulness is calmness, which is the state in which you are best placed to deal with challenges. If you're with a toxic person you're going to face plenty of those.

Like relaxation techniques, mindfulness takes practice. Do get one of the books I've mentioned, go to some mindfulness classes, get a mindfulness audio file or whatever. But stick at it.

Dealing with gameplaying

You might find it worth glancing back at the section on game-playing in Chapter 2 at this stage, unless your memory is a lot better than mine. I'm including the subject here rather than in the next chapter because it isn't only habitual gameplayers who use this manoeuvre. Most toxic people also do so, though maybe less often than dyed-in-the-wool gameplayers.

If you often feel you've been put in a position where you're not comfortable, but are unable quite to put your finger on why you're uncomfortable or how to refuse or protest without seeming unreasonable, the chances are that you're embroiled in someone's game. The point about games is that they are covert, subtle, not obvious, particularly to outsiders. But they are carefully designed to make you do what you wouldn't do by choice.

People play games because of the payoff they get from doing so, that is the reward for successfully using the tactic. So you need to understand what the player is doing and what her payoff is. That's why the study of gameplaying is called 'transactional analysis'. You need to understand the transaction, what is really going on, and its purpose. When you've achieved this, it's time to design the *antithesis*, that is the measure you take to prevent the player from achieving her desired payoff.

Let's go back to Helen and her mother, from the introduction and the gameplaying section in Chapter 2. Mum recognizes that Helen has little self-esteem and less sense of entitlement. After all, her neglectful and abusive parenting made Helen that way. She uses these vulnerabilities, playing on Helen's guilt. Mum's payoffs are the power to bend Helen to her will, ensuring Helen's company without having to be kind in return, placing herself in front of Helen's husband and friends in the pecking order of importance, and saving money. So what are the antitheses? Think about this for a minute. I have my ideas, but it's good practice for you to form your own.

For me, Helen should start by giving up the myth that, if she tries hard enough and is a good enough daughter, her mother one day will express her love and appreciation. No she won't. If she was going to do that, she would have done it 30 years ago. So Helen should make it very clear to Mum what she will and won't do, and when Mum tries to make her feel guilty she should refuse to acknowledge any guilt, even if she feels it. That is an antithesis; Mum won't be getting her payoff for playing the 'I'll make you guilty' game. When Mum fails to attend her hospital appointment, 'because I couldn't face it without you there to support me', Helen should shrug her shoulders and respond, 'Oh, well, you'd better rebook, hadn't you? Get your neighbour Phyllis to take you if you want company.'

Mum will be horrified, will go quiet for a few days or weeks, and then Helen will get a call from Phyllis to say that Mum isn't eating well, is going downhill, and what is Helen going to do about it? Be careful now, Helen, you're being sucked back into the game. Ask Phyllis to phone Mum's GP or suggest Mum do so herself. But don't go round and sort everything out. Ardent gameplayers will keep the struggle to bend you to their will going for some time. It isn't uncommon for the Helens of this world to receive phone calls from Mum or from a neighbour saying that Mum has taken an overdose of medicine. I can't say there is no risk to Helen standing her ground, but I can say this: the risk is much greater if she doesn't. If Mum continues to succeed in getting her payoff by raising the stakes, she is likely to keep doing so every time Helen tries to impose limits. Deciding on an appropriate limit (it's helpful to talk to friends and loved ones about this) and sticking to it is the least risky option.

This may all seem rather hard and cruel, but it isn't. I'm not suggesting that Helen should turn from a doting daughter into a hard, heartless, self-centred curmudgeon. I do, though, believe that she should treat herself as of equal importance with her mother; not more important, but not less so either. Her duties should be balanced between her mother's needs and her own, and in order to achieve that balance she's going to have to understand her mother's games and employ some antitheses. Read Eric Berne's *Games People Play* if you need more help with this.

The principle of treating everyone as of equal importance is explored further in the book *I'm OK, You're OK* by Thomas Harris. The premise is well encapsulated in the title. If your starting point is not that you have to disprove your hypothesis that you are worthless or prove that you are better than the next person, but that we're all OK despite our differences, your vulnerability to gameplaying and manipulation is greatly diminished. No need for judgements of your own or others' worth, just freedom to make your own decisions.

This stuff is hard. Lifetime gameplayers are very skilled at what they do. Don't expect to turn it all around in an instant. But do think about what is going on, the payoffs and the possible antitheses, and talk about them to people who really care about you.

11

Coping with specific types of toxic people

The principles I have outlined in the last three chapters should help you cope with whatever type of toxicity you face, but it's worth going back to the types of people and situations who or which tend to do harm, to make sure we're clear on what you need to do to cope with them. I'll refer to the same characters who illustrated the different types of toxic people in Chapter 4. Look back to that chapter if you need to.

Boundary invaders

George's nature will be clear fairly quickly after you meet him. His audacity is remarkable. So beware from the outset. The easiest way to set boundaries with him is at the beginning. If you refuse to be persuaded by him, he'll turn to someone else who is easier to push around. Be firm and consistent. If he labels you as a selfish person and a bad friend because you won't give in to him, so what? Better than being his slave.

If you've known George for months or years and you aren't a naturally assertive person, the chances are that George has already achieved a shifting of your boundaries, which he has taken as the new norm. You're the one who always says yes, does what is asked of you, lends him money and doesn't get repaid. Shifting these boundaries back to where you want them is harder than it would have been if you'd set them in stone to begin with, but it's not impossible. Be honest and clear. Don't make up excuses, as he'll see through them or find a way of invalidating them. 'No George, not today, I'm tired and I don't feel like it' (presuming you are tired – if you're not, don't pretend, just say no) will be met with horrified incredulity, but stick to your guns. 'Oh, come on, just this once, it's really important' can be countered with a simple shake of the head and a straight 'No, not today,' whereas if you had spun some yarn to get you out of whatever he was asking things would have been much more complicated. You'd be operating in George's wheelhouse; he's very good at finding ways past excuses.

If you want to take this opportunity to draw a line in the sand, by all means do so, perhaps by saying, 'George, by all means ask me for stuff, but please don't count on me saying yes. I want a choice.' But if you don't feel up to confronting him in this way right now, no matter, so long as from now on you're consistent with your boundaries. He'll eventually get the message and test somebody else's boundaries instead.

Nuclei of chaos

If Mildred is your friend or acquaintance, keep a safe distance and don't get pulled into taking responsibility for her. To an extent, the same holds true for family members, though the parents of underage children or those with a mental illness are in a more diffi-cult situation, as are spouses. Wherever possible, Mildred should be left in no doubt that she is responsible for her actions and that you aren't going to take responsibility for them. Do this from the start of your relationship or friendship, whenever Mildred does anything that feels destructive and over the top (her behaviours may not be extraordinary at first, but they will tend to escalate). This really is crucial. If Mildred comes to rely on you bailing her out so that she can avoid the consequences of her excesses, the risk that she will act irresponsibly is increased.

I have to admit, though, that this can be really hard. One of the most difficult aspects of my job was maintaining this boundary with the Mildreds under my care. It took a lot of nerve, when one particular Mildred (I should emphasize that the exact details of what happened in this case have been changed) phoned me from her mobile to tell me that she was standing on a window ledge, not to go screeching around to where she was and haul her to safety. More than once in this type of situation I refused to call the police or go to the scene myself, but firmly told my patient to get back inside and then phone me back to arrange an urgent appointment. But I can tell you, it took a lot out of me.

Presuming you're not a mental health professional, these judgement calls will be even harder, and of course, you have to err on the side of safety. But remember that always being Mildred's saviour isn't likely to make her safer in the long run. Don't allow yourself to be a puppet on the end of Mildred's string. If Mildred really is as chaotic as described in Chapter 4, try to get her to see a psychiatrist if you can. Or even better, if you're not related to Mildred, try to have somebody else, preferably a family member, take her.

If it's down to you, this will mean you getting her to her GP first. And you'll need to go with her, as at first glance there will be nothing to indicate the turmoil under Mildred's surface. If, say, after taking some pills, she ends up in A&E, try to have a word with the attending doctor if you can. If Mildred has a contact point in her local community mental health team, you'll be off the hook to an extent at her many times of crisis. As always, don't allow yourself to become isolated. Talk to wise friends and family in order to seek guidance when you can, and to a doctor when expertise is required. Above all, give yourself recognition for what you're trying to do. You are in a horribly difficult situation, one in which nobody gets it right all the time. Try to change the way you react to Mildred's drama and chaos, but don't expect to become expert at managing her excesses overnight. If you feel that you need some therapy yourself to help you cope, why not? Start by going to your GP and see what he or she has to say.

Users, abusers, loafers and energy vampires

I really can't see the point in hanging around a user, even less an abuser. If you can, fair enough; maybe you're married to Joel. I'm certainly not going to advocate divorce, unless that's what you've already decided on. But, if marriage isn't the reason, you do need to ask yourself why Joel is in your life. Do you have a set of assumptions or 'givens' that are keeping you in the destructive relationship? If you assume that your role in life is always to serve others regardless of how they treat you, I would dispute your assumption. Life is about giving and taking; the two need to be in balance.

Tell Joel what your needs are. He may not realize and, being a bloke, he may need telling several times. Most men aren't very intuitive. But if Joel wilfully and persistently ignores your needs you really need to consider what your relationship with him is for. Hoping that he'll change and become kinder with time is pointless. It isn't going to happen. If you cross Joel off your list of friends, you may be lonely for a while, particularly if you lead quite a solitary life, but I would suggest that a fake friend is worse than no friend at all. Once you get the Joels out of your life other, more giving people will find you, if you let them. It may take some time, but it will happen. Real friends haven't appeared before now because there was no space for them; Joel took it all.

Joel the loafer needs to be given instructions as to what you require from him, in words of one syllable. Make it specific. There's no point asking him to be kinder or more respectful, to do more or be less selfish. He won't know what you mean. Work out what your bottom line is, the minimum which may make Joel a worthwhile friend or partner, such as: 'I need you to tell me something nice about me at least once a day when you're with me, to say thank you when I make you a cup of coffee, to pay for meals out half the time and not to insult me in public.' Even with injunctions this specific, some fine tuning may be necessary. For example, Joel may have different standards from yours regarding what constitutes an insult. He may forget or lapse into old behaviours and need reminding. Equally, he may need pointers about what constitutes a compliment. But stick with it and be consistent; it's the only chance your friendship or relationship has. If Joel simply refuses to change, he's an abuser. Remind me again why you're hanging around?

Joel the energy vampire needs equally frank feedback. Don't just sit and seethe at his 'yes but'-ing. Tell him that you have reached your limit with hearing about his woes, unless he's going to do something about them. You'll feel like a bad friend, but you're not, otherwise Joel wouldn't have selected you. You're just setting a boundary. You're being honest about your limits and giving him the privilege of being told what they are before you become angry or resentful. Better for both you and Joel in the long run. Again, if Joel just can't or won't change, consider your options.

If you're married to one of these Joels you have my sympathy. That's not going to help you though. What might is decisive action. First, don't be a victim. An abusive relationship requires the assumption of roles, one of perpetrator and the other of victim. I'm reminded of a Renaissance fresco in an Italian church of a martyr facing torture with beatific resignation: the saintly victim facing his abuser with stoic aplomb. But hang on, is this really what you choose? If it isn't, do something. Take responsibility for improving your lot. If you do things for Joel, make them contingent on him treating you properly. Define what your needs are, what you'll do if they're met and what you'll change if they aren't. Try to look at what you're asking from Joel's point of view. Are you confident it's reasonable? If you are, but Joel is angered by what you say, consider whatever point he makes and negotiate if appropriate, but try not to let yourself be bullied out of what you really need; you're only storing up problems for the future if you do.

Very occasionally, spouses have to put their foot down and insist on joint marital counselling (such as is available through Relate). If it gets to this point, don't ask Joel, tell him. Joel isn't going to vote for joint counselling as the status quo suits him just fine, or he thinks it does. You may have to demand it as a condition of you staying together. Be careful though; what will you do if Joel refuses? If he calls your bluff and you don't carry through on your threat, the chances of anything changing will disappear completely.

Bullies and sadists

As I pointed out in Chapter 4, there really isn't much you can do with a bully or a sadist, as they will be better at bullying than you are at resisting unless you are a very confident and assertive person. If you have real evidence from your experience that Clive is a bully or a sadist, get away from him. I don't mean you need to abandon a relationship if your friend or partner is having an off day and snaps at you once. But if Clive repeatedly hurts or humiliates you, he'll keep doing so. When you say you're going to leave he'll try to reel you back in with promises that he'll change, but he won't, not for long, unless he does something real to achieve this change, such as getting into therapy.

If you move out, don't go back until you feel comfortable to do so, and until you're really confident that Clive's change is real and permanent. Clive will tell you that he can't get by or make progress in treatment without you, but once more this is him trying to regain control, to reel you back in. Be firm and consistent. If you don't believe that Clive is really changing, don't be rushed, and if necessary don't go back. He will try to persuade you that nobody else will have you, that you need him. No you don't. It's better to be alone than to be a victim. There are a lot of kind and loving people out there, though Clive will try to persuade you that there aren't. Bullying isn't the norm and it isn't right, whatever Clive says.

Bombs and bombasts

Don't try to remonstrate with Sarah when she's engaged in a fit of temper. She's out of control and unreachable by logic. If a machine gun is spinning round and spewing out bullets at random it's better not to be in the vicinity. Quietly and politely remove yourself, if necessary explaining that you'll be happy to discuss the issue later. When later comes, likely as not Sarah will have forgotten all about it. She's let off steam and now isn't bothered with what it was all about.

But it is important, if Sarah is a friend or partner, that you return to the issue when she has calmed down, for at least two reasons. First, her temper tantrum will have prevented the issue being adequately discussed or any real exchange of information from taking place. Once Sarah is calm these can be achieved. Second, there's an opportunity for feedback. It's worth telling Sarah how her outburst made you feel, perhaps by saying: 'Sarah, I know you didn't mean to upset me, but when you got angry I found it quite scary and upsetting. Please don't shout at me, OK?' If she's honest, Sarah won't be able to promise this, as her tantrums take her by surprise as much as they do you, but at least you've established your existence as someone whose feelings matter.

You need to be even clearer with Sarah the bombast. Say it straight and clear, in words of one syllable. You might be upset if someone spoke so frankly to you, but Sarah is very unlikely to be so sensitive. After all, that's why she acts like she does: she lacks sensitivity. Don't treat her as you'd like to be treated, but as she treats others. Be as blunt as you like, though you should try to stay kind, reasonable and focused on the point you want to get across. So to Sarah, it's OK to say: 'Please don't keep telling me what to do. I know more about widgets than you do. I don't want your advice on this, OK?' That would sound a bit harsh to someone else, but not to Sarah.

You'll notice that again I've finished the sentence in your response to Sarah with 'OK?' This is quite a useful device, as it invites either agreement or the flagging up of any area of disagreement or misunderstanding, which you can then deal with.

Have this discussion with Sarah, if possible, in private. If there are others around it may induce her to grandstand argumentatively. She's much more likely to accept your boundary one to one.

Bigots, blowhards, fundamentalists and zealots

I really don't know what to do with these types. If I did I'd have a job with a number of governments negotiating with the Taliban and ISIS. If you can find an area of common interest with Donald, do so, but keep away from any contentious areas. Just because Donald demands to know your views on this or that doesn't mean you have to tell him. It's OK to say, 'You know, Donald, that's something I don't want to discuss.'

'Oh, so you're some kind of Commie, are you, then?' replies Donald.

'No, I'm not, but I'm not going to discuss politics with you.'

Stick to your guns on this. If it proves impossible, you may need to give Donald a wide berth. There's certainly no chance of you changing his mind on anything or having a reasonable exchange of views. Donald is what he is, and if that doesn't suit you, find a different friend. If he dominates your friendship group, you may end up losing some of them as friends too, but really that is up to them. Hanging around with Donald isn't going to make for a happy life, unless, that is, you are prepared to agree with all of his prejudices.

Narcissists

With Elizabeth it's all about limits. Her needs have no limits, but your task is to set limits on her expectations. Decide how far Elizabeth can go with you and then make the limit clear to her. Is it OK for her to take credit at work for something for which you put in most of the effort? Is it OK for her to show off to you all the time? How much of your time and emotional energy are you willing to give her? Remember, Elizabeth has no intrinsic sense of self-worth, and she's constantly looking to you and others to affirm her through your praise, support and attention. It really isn't her fault she's like this – it's because she didn't receive the praise, attention and support she needed as a child – but that doesn't change the fact that her demands on you will increase the more you give. As a kind and giving person, that makes you vulnerable to being sucked dry by Elizabeth's needs.

Once you identify Elizabeth's neediness, decide what you will and won't be for her. If that doesn't include being the one who does the work she takes credit for, make this crystal clear right now. Set the boundary clearly and quickly. When you've had enough of her self-aggrandizing stories, tell her so, as kindly as you can manage. You're responsible for setting a boundary as clearly and kindly as you can, not for how Elizabeth reacts to it. Make it clear from the outset what you will and won't do for her, and let her be disappointed in you for not doing more. You may not have been Elizabeth's perfect saviour, but by tolerating her neediness while setting clear limits, you've done a lot for her; and you've avoided becoming overwhelmed and angry, and thus perpetuating the pattern of rejection which has been her life so far.

If you keep meeting Elizabeths and find yourself surrounded by them, you should look at the signals you're giving off through your generosity and attentiveness. If the impression you give people is 'I'm here for you no matter what and I'll always give you whatever you ask for', you need to work on your boundaries and limit-setting. You can be a kind person without having 'mug' printed on your forehead. Talk to friends who are better than you at being firm and looking after themselves about how to achieve this.

Psychopaths/sociopaths

Don't go there if you have the option. Alex is bad news, really bad, and he'll hurt you. As soon as you realize that Alex has no real feelings for you or for anyone else, no conscience and no compunction in doing whatever it takes to get what he wants, put as much distance between the two of you as you can. If you work with him, that means erecting a cool, professional and effective boundary. 'I'm not your enemy, but don't mess with me or try to push me around because it won't work' is the message you need to get across. If you think he's your friend, he isn't; get away. If you're married to him, talk to your friends for support. A lot. Maybe seek the support of a counsellor or psychotherapist. And remember that you have a say in how you live your life.

Alex has no better nature, so don't try appealing to it. Just be very vigilant, considered and strategic in your dealings with him. You wouldn't turn your back on a hungry wolf; don't turn your back on Alex either (I'm talking metaphorically). Don't try to teach him a lesson or get one over on him. He's better at it than you are. But, as with so many other toxic people, you can and you must maintain your boundaries. You don't have to do what you don't want to do, just because Alex tells you to.

Paranoid possessors

Here, a degree of judgement is needed. Some insecurity is a normal part of a loving relationship, as are misunderstandings and requests for reassurance and clarification, but when Mary's insecurity utterly dominates every facet of your relationship, you need to take action. Don't allow yourself to suffer house arrest in an effort to avoid upsetting her. Don't engage in long cross-examinations to prove your fidelity. Set a reasonable limit on how far it's acceptable for her to check on you. If Mary cannot be placated or convinced of your faithfulness, don't keep increasing your efforts to prove it. At some point you'll have to put your foot down, and it might as well be now. Mary's problems cannot be fixed by your efforts. She needs to deal with her insecurity and the lack of confidence that underpins it, and this may mean getting some professional help. If you can solve the issue by talking it through frankly, agreeing on limits and reasonable steps to reassure Mary, all well and good, but if not, your relationship is unlikely to survive without such help.

This, of course, assumes that you have never been guilty of infidelity. If you have, don't ask or expect Mary to trust you until she is ready. Welcome any demand to check on you, within reason. Your emails, texts, bank statements and phone records are Mary's property until further notice. You gave up your right to privacy when you cheated on her.

What is the definition of infidelity? Does it include a drunken kiss with your neighbour's wife at a party? You and Mary will have to decide on that between the two of you, but if you've been indiscreet, wait for Mary's trust to return, don't demand it.

If, in contrast, Mary's insecurity and possessiveness has crossed the boundary into delusional (morbid) jealousy (see Chapter 4), you are at some risk. If you are really clear that this is happening, particularly if Mary's accusations have led to her becoming violent, this is the one situation in which I would advise you to leave and to stay away until she has received effective treatment for her condition. If you are in doubt, seek the advice of a professional, which in the first instance means going to see your GP.

Doubters and avoiders

The key to William the obsessional doubter is that doubting is what he is. Unless he gets effective treatment, he will never change. Once you've been through a couple of cycles with him of being courted and rejected you need to accept that this is who he is. Decide whether this is the life you choose. If not, heartbreak and loneliness are temporary; William's cycles are for ever. Face up to that now and you've awarded yourself a life. If William gets treatment, great. Change can happen, even with the most entrenched obsessional doubters, given time, effort and a good therapist, but look for evidence of real and persisting change, rather than relying on William's assurances.

As with so many of the people who populate this chapter, the most important principle for coping with William the phobic avoider is to set firm and consistent limits. Yes, by all means improve your standards of cleanliness and hygiene, but only up to a reasonable limit (seek the advice of friends if you need to). Don't allow yourself to be co-opted into meaningless rituals. This may lead to a crisis and an upsetting argument, but you need to stand your ground now, or your life, like William's, will become totally dominated by his phobias and associated rituals. If William needs treatment because of the effect his problems are having on him, on you, or particularly on your children, insist on it. Be as firm as you can on this. An argument now may save a world of distress down the line.

Scorekeepers

I think that the key with Izzy isn't managing her, but yourself. You can never satisfy Izzy, unless you undergo surgery to join yourself to her at the hip. Problems will arise if you expect yourself to keep her happy. This will only lead to you becoming exhausted, unhappy and demoralized, as you will fail. So accept the failure, in fact rejoice in it. By letting Izzy hold her own unhappiness rather than taking it on yourself you are freeing yourself of the yoke of her expectations. Presuming that she has some redeeming features which lead you to want to maintain contact with her, the question of whether she keeps you as a friend is for Izzy to answer, not you. She'll need to accept you as you are, limits and all. She can harrumph all she likes; you'll sweep her disapproval aside with a breezy shrug and a smile, because you're only going to give what you choose to give. Take it or leave it.

Accepting that I won't make everyone happy all the time and that sometimes people won't like or approve of me has been the most liberating achievement of my life. I hope that you too can achieve this acceptance.

Jokers and storytellers

Bill is funny and engaging, which makes it easy to be taken in by him. But remember that Bill's weapon is his audience. Do you want to be part of the truncheon with which he beats his victim? When he's telling a joke or teasing someone else, consider how you'd feel if you were the object of his humour. If you're not a confident person, it's not worth calling Bill out on his cruelty lest he turn his fire on you, though if you are and you enjoy a verbal joust, by all means do so. Otherwise, quietly and without fuss, remove yourself from Bill's orbit. Don't listen to his stories or jokes about people. Find something to do which allows you to escape the situation.

If you're in Bill's cross-hairs, bad luck. Again, get out of the situation as quickly as you can. In my experience, a bored 'Yeah, yeah, whatever. Funny one, Bill' as you walk away is as effective an exit strategy as any. Getting upset or angry only plays into his hands. Be upset later, in private, or in the company of supportive friends. You won't be the first to have been humiliated by Bill. His other victims can be a valuable source of mutual support.

Addicts

I'll deal with Sally the alcoholic here, though the principles are the same whatever the addiction. If you want more detail on this subject you could turn to my book *Dying for a Drink*, or even better find a local meeting of Al-Anon, the sister organization to Alcoholics Anonymous for the family members of people suffering from alcoholism. (Families Anonymous is the equivalent organization for the family members of people addicted to drugs.)

First, what not to do. Don't become part of the pattern of addiction. Don't cover for the addict, make excuses for her, justify her behaviour, protect her, save her from the consequences of her actions. Don't allow your needs to be sidelined or yourself to be silenced in order to enjoy an easy life. Don't try to remonstrate or have a meaningful conversation with someone who is intoxicated. You're talking to the drink, not the person, who in any case won't remember a word of what was said the next morning. But equally, don't sweep anything under the carpet.

If Sally has abused you when drunk, you need to point this out to her the next day before she starts drinking and make it clear that abuse is unacceptable to you. Be tough. It isn't loving to let things slide by staying silent; if you do you're colluding in the pattern of addiction. Al-Anon talk a lot about 'tough love', and they're right. If you love Sally, be as hard as nails about her drinking. No compromise, no turning a blind eye, no ignoring a small lapse, just very firm boundaries. There are some experts who would disagree, but my view is that anybody who has been addicted to a substance or behaviour can never again hope to return to controlled use of it. That means that Sally needs to abstain totally and permanently from alcohol. She will also need help, maybe from an addiction specialist or a self-help group. As far as I'm concerned, the best of these is AA, which is free and available in almost every major town in the UK. Suggest that Sally phone the AA national helpline (0800 9177 650) or visit their website. She'll be given the details of a meeting in her area, and if she phones may be given a contact person who will take Sally to her first meeting. You'll need to be very firm, as the phenomena of denial, minimization, rationalization and blaming others are symptoms of the disease of addiction. Al-Anon will give you the support you need in standing firm.

Active alcoholics tend to be very crafty and expert at hiding their drinking. But if you're honest with yourself, you know how Sally behaves when she's drunk. If she's acting that way after a period of being back to her old self, she has probably relapsed. If you want to, look for empty bottles lying around or in the bin. Don't trust her word on her sobriety. If Sally were my patient I would tell her not to expect your trust until she's got at least two years' sobriety under her belt. Not only should she not expect you to trust her, she shouldn't trust herself either. That isn't any criticism of Sally, it's a recognition of the overwhelming power of addiction. Don't for a moment, though, think that you can stop Sally from drinking. Lock an active alcoholic in a steel vault with walls ten feet thick and watch her find a way out to get to a drink.

Addiction is a giant mega-tsunami, 100 feet high. A man stands on a beach and watches the wave approaching. He looks it up and down and declares, 'Yes, I can handle that.' What? Are you mad? Of course you can't handle it, it's a force of nature, you'll be swept away. Run for the hills.

AA is the high ground for Sally. Al-Anon is yours. Try not to be jealous of the time she's spending at meetings. It is an investment in the future for you both. The good news is that if Sally establishes a real recovery from her addiction, she will no longer be toxic. Indeed, the chances are that with the help of the 12-step process, she'll become a better person than she ever was before. As I observed in Chapter 4, many of the world's best people are addicts in recovery.

12

What if I'm toxic?

As I explained in Chapter 4, if you think you may be toxic I doubt whether you are, because most people who are toxic are unaware of their toxicity, or are very resistant to recognizing it. If they were aware of it and cared about it, they probably would have changed by now. The majority of people who consulted me because they felt they were harming those around them turned out to be suffering from major depression, or depressive illness. Their negative judgements about themselves were a product of the distorted perception and thinking which were symptoms of their illness. So if you think you're toxic, first go to see your GP to be checked out for depression. Treatment (with medications, CBT, or a combination of the two) is usually successful, and it will change everything, particularly how you see yourself.

But let's proceed with the assumption that you are an exception, that you tend to cause harm to others and you really want to change. Bear in mind the following points:

1 It isn't your fault. Everyone is the way he is for a reason, usually reflecting his life experiences and (to a lesser extent) his genetics. Stop beating yourself up and start looking for ways to change.
2 You aren't a bad person. Making negative value judgements about yourself doesn't help. Positive action does. Focus on the behaviours you want to change.
3 Take responsibility. What happened before you realized you had a choice to change wasn't your fault, but now you know more, which gives you a responsibility to change how you act towards the people you affect the most.
4 Understand yourself. This book, particularly Part I, may help you to understand how you tick, and why. Are the issues that made you the way you are ones which you can deal with? If not, seek some help. There's no shame in that. Many of the world's

greatest figures have needed psychotherapy at some point in their lives. Start by telling your GP that you want some counselling or psychotherapy. Your GP will know where to get this help.

5 You can change. Personality isn't set in stone, it changes over time and with different ways of being. You become the way you act, so decide how you would like to be and start acting that way. This will make you feel like a fraud at the outset, but stick with it. You're acting for now, but in due course, with persistence, it will become the real you. If you want to be kinder, look for opportunities to act kindly. It doesn't matter how you feel about it, just do it. Repeatedly, for as long as it takes to feel kind.

You may need some help with this, for example, if you are prone to explosive temper. The explosion happens before you've had time to plan what to do. You'll need a therapist (clinical psychologists tend to be particularly good at helping people to change behaviours) to give you some pointers for recognizing the warning signs, and for developing strategies for what to do when they occur.

6 Talk regularly to somebody you can trust. If that's the person you feel you've harmed, so much the better, but he may not be able to give you accurate information about his needs or what he wants you to change, because of lack of perception or confidence. Resist the urge to coerce him into reassuring you, as he'll probably be all too ready to do so to placate you, but his reassurance isn't reliable and by demanding it you're only compounding your dominance over him and his welfare.

If you have a wise friend or family member whom you feel would give you truthful feedback and advice, talk to that person. Listen to him or her. Try to say less and hear more. If you're at your wits' end and don't know what to do, seek professional advice. Again, start with your GP.

7 Give yourself time, patience and understanding. It has taken your whole life to get this way. It's going to take a while to turn it around. You'll trip up along the way, that's natural. When you do, don't berate yourself, but be honest about your lapse, with yourself and your loved ones, and learn from it.

8 Finally, don't look for applause. Change is its own reward. Those you have affected may well not acknowledge what has occurred,

or may be unable to express it to you. Even if they are, they may be unable to forgive you on demand. The road you've travelled has been long and rough for you; it has been the same for them. But if you made a choice to change and have carried it through, make no mistake, you've done a wonderful thing. If you can spot a toxic pattern going back through the generations in your family and you have changed it for the first time, you have turned around for the better the future of countless generations to come. If that's not wonderful, I don't know what is.

Conclusion

So where are we with this? We've considered how people tick, why they behave the way they do, both individually and in groups, including families, and how they can be influenced. Then we looked at some of the different types of toxic people, places and situations you may encounter, and we spent some time with toxic families. Finally, we built on this knowledge to work out strategies for dealing with toxicity, including general principles which are useful whatever type of toxicity you are facing and the specific action necessary to manage the different types of toxic people, places, situations or families you may face. You have learned a relaxation exercise, though it's going to take quite a lot of practice before you're good enough at it for it to be useful in the heat of battle. You know the principles of mindfulness, but are going to need to read some more about it before it too is really useful. Likewise the transactional analysis of gameplaying and how to administer effective antitheses to stop the games harming you. But in Chapter 12, we also identified specific actions you can take to address toxic people in your life right now.

So now you can start using this knowledge to change the way you interact with the world and in particular the people who have been affecting you in a negative way. This will mean challenging a lot of your attitudes and preconceptions about how you should behave. This won't be comfortable, but then nothing new ever is. A few years ago I met a young man in his late thirties on a golf course and got talking with him. He was a city trader and was highly successful at it. He was very good at golf and I asked him how he had become so skilful. He told me that up until five years previously he had been a golf teaching professional. 'What made you change careers? The money?' I asked.

'No,' he replied, 'I just couldn't cope with my pupils any more. I would tell them what to do to fix their golf swing, then they'd come back a week later swinging the same weird way they always had. I would ask them why they hadn't taken my advice and they'd reply that they hadn't persevered because the new swing was uncomfortable. One day I snapped and told my pupil that he should go away and keep playing comfortably bad golf and stop wasting his money on me. I knew then that it was time for a career change.'

He was right, and was very fortunate that he did. I kind of know how he felt. If you don't take charge of your life and make some major changes in the way you relate to the people you experience as toxic, everything will remain the same. Don't blame the architect of your misery for how you feel. It's not them, it's you. They're just being the way they always have been and it suits them just fine. It's you who have to shake things up if you want your life to get better.

You will have noticed several repeating themes in this book, prime among them being the importance of treating yourself with the same understanding and respect you accord to others. Second in importance is seeking support. Reach out to friends when you need them. Don't let yourself be isolated. If you need professional help, go to your GP as your first port of call. Running a close third in importance is being strategic, seeking opportunity rather than fairness. Use your brain rather than your emotions to deal with the problems you face. Understanding and planning are a lot more use to you than righteous indignation.

If everything you've learnt from this book isn't enough to protect you from someone's toxic effect on you, it's time for you to say goodbye to them (although marriage may be an exception; see Chapter 9). Some toxic people are better at being toxic than you'll ever be at resisting them. In that case, an emptier address book and some temporary loneliness is in my view better than being oppressed. Good people tend to turn up in your life when there is space for them. There is no space when you're in the grip of toxic people. In any case, what I've found time and again is that people, whether friends or life partners, tend to turn up just when you don't need them. When you start recognizing that you're an OK person and are all right on your own, good people magically arrive in your life. It's one of life's many ironies. Of course, it's not really magic. Confidence and self-esteem are very attractive to good people (and equally repellent to toxic people who would use and abuse you).

So to end, let's return to Helen (see Introduction and Chapter 10). What could she do differently?

Start by dropping the excuses. They give the wrong message, which is that she would do anything possible to help her friend Anita. Where's her choice? Try a different tack:

'No Anita, not today. I've got a lot on and I really don't want to overstretch myself and get tired.'

'Oh, go on, just this once, I really need this evening out.'

Helen fixes Anita with a steely gaze. 'No, I'm sad that you're disappointed in me, but as I said, not today.' (Note here that Helen doesn't say 'I'm sorry I disappointed you'. This isn't an apology, it is expressing disappointment at Anita's reaction. Helen didn't actively disappoint Anita; Anita chose to be disappointed.)

'Well, I am disappointed actually. I would have thought you could have done more for your best friend.'

'Yes, I'm sure you would. Anyway, let's talk about something else. How was your visit to the gym today?' (There is no effort to defend or excuse here, just a firm digging in of heels.)

Anita will sulk for a while, but she'll get over it and a boundary has been set which Helen can build on in the future. If Anita doesn't get over it, she isn't a friend and Helen's address book will be lighter and better without Anita's name in it.

Mum next. I've suggested a pattern for Helen's interaction with her mum in Chapter 10, but let's rehearse it again. There are several effective variations on this theme.

'Look Mum, I'm not going to take you to your appointment today because I have too much on. Here's the number of an excellent local taxi service for you to call. I can also install the Uber app on your phone.'

'Well, I don't know what the world's coming to when a mother can't even turn to her daughter when she's ill. After everything I've done for you.'

'Yes, well there it is. I'll be around at the weekend to help you with the curtains, if you want me to of course.' (Again, a firm refusal to shift the boundary Helen has set.)

'Oh, don't bother. I'm sure I'm not important enough to fit into your busy schedule.'

'OK then. Phone me when you need anything.' (Refusal to take the bait and play the guilt game.)

Helen's mother phones the next day and says she missed the

appointment because she couldn't face it without Helen. As I recommended in Chapter 10, Helen responds that her mother should rebook the appointment, taking her neighbour Phyllis with her if she wants company.

'Oh, I don't like phoning, would you do it for me dear?'

'No Mum, you need to do it yourself. I haven't got your diary in front of me.'

Helen then won't get a call for two weeks, having previously had one every day, and her mother won't answer her phone. Then Phyllis will phone to say that her mother has 'had a turn' and been taken to hospital by ambulance, explaining that Helen needs to come over urgently, as her mother needs her. It transpires that she was released from A&E after being examined, with no diagnosis other than slightly high blood pressure because she had run out of her pills a week ago.

'Thanks Phyllis. Tell Mum to give me a call and I'll see what she needs.' (Putting the emphasis on Mum taking action rather than running after her.)

Still no call. Now, this is when Helen needs to gird her loins and dig in. She has identified her mother's game and the antithesis, which is to remove the reward for her mother's manipulations by refusing to be always at her beck and call. Sooner or later Mum will call.

'Oh, I haven't seen you for ages. I've been so lonely and I'm very unwell.'

'Oh dear, sorry to hear that, Mum. I can come around on Saturday if you like.' (No apology, no promise to fix Mum's feelings.)

Antithesis delivered, control regained. Lots of guilt feelings, but they will pass, unlike the exhaustion and desperation which was Helen's life previously. I can't guarantee that nothing bad will happen during Mum's ratcheting up of the stakes in her effort to make Helen feel guilty and to force her compliance, but it's less risky to make a stand now than to let the gameplaying continue. If Helen is unsure about this, she should turn to wise friends for guidance, or even if necessary seek counselling or psychotherapy.

Finally, Helen turns the cross-hairs on Edward. When he gets home late probably isn't the best time, so she leaves it for now, but at least there's no row about their daughter being kept up late as there would have been had Anita's son been in her charge all evening. She waits until the next morning, then arranges a time with Edward for them to have a talk about how things are organized. They agree on Saturday afternoon, when their daughter is at their neighbour's on a play date. Edward suggested Saturday evening for their discussion, but Helen wisely turned down that suggestion, as Edward starts drinking at 5 p.m. on Saturday and gets argumentative when he's had a few.

When the time comes, Helen opens with 'Edward, I've been thinking, I'm not happy with doing everything around the house. I'd like you to take on at least one of the chores, please.'

'Why? I work my guts out at work and I deserve some rest when I get home.'

'Yes, you do, I agree, but I'm exhausted all the time and I would feel a lot better if you contributed a bit at home.' (No argument about who does more, no right-fighting, just a dogged refusal to be deflected.)

'Oh, for goodness sake, do I have to do everything?'

'No, but I thought you could be responsible for putting the rubbish out and taking our daughter out on Saturday afternoons so that I can have a rest.' (Effective refusal to be drawn into a slanging match in response to Edward's provocative use of hyperbole.)

'But that's when I watch the football.'

'You can record it. Unless you've got another suggestion.' (Well-planned response to Edward's predictable objection.)

And so the negotiation goes on. In the end Edward, after some huffing and puffing, concedes, and Helen gets one task handed over and an hour a week to herself. Edward is resentful but he'll get over it. Helen's foot is in the door and now she'll start to feel she can negotiate on other issues too.

Helen feels worried and horribly guilty for being demanding and letting everyone down. She shouldn't worry about these feelings (don't worry about worrying), as they are an indication she's going in the right direction. She fights against her urge to put herself last, as she now realizes that she is entitled to the same consideration as the next person. Not more, not less, just the same. She's traded long-term exhaustion, resentment, unhappiness and illness for a bit of short-term worry and guilt. She deals with these troublesome emotions by practising her relaxation and mindfulness exercises. In any case, being able to share with caring friends about what she has done leads to her receiving a great deal of reassurance and affirmation that she's doing the right things.

Helen has just awarded herself a life. I for one am overjoyed for her. Go girl! Keep it up!

Further reading

Eric Berne, *Games People Play* (London: Penguin, 1987)
Dr Tim Cantopher, *Dying for a Drink* (London: Sheldon Press, 2011)
Dr Tim Cantopher, *Stress-related Illness* (London: Sheldon Press, 2007)
Max Ehrmann, 'Desiderata' (poem, available online)
Victor Frankl, *Man's Search for Meaning* (Boston, MA: Beacon Press, 2006)
Thomas Harris, *I'm OK, You're OK* (London: Arrow, 2012)
Jon Kabat-Zinn, *Wherever You Go, There You Are: Mindfulness meditation for everyday life* (London: Piatkus, 2004)
Robin Skynner and John Cleese, *Families and How to Survive Them* (London: Cedar Books, new edition 1993)
Mark Williams and Danny Penman, *Mindfulness: A practical guide to finding peace in a frantic world* (London: Piatkus, 2011)
Janet Woititz, *Adult Children of Alcoholics* (Deerfield Beach, FL: Health Communications, 1990)

Index